BUILDING HEALTHY RELATIONSHIPS IN EARLY LEARNING

MACOMB FAMILY SERVICES' APPROACH
TO NURTURING DEVELOPMENT OF SOCIAL
EMOTIONAL HEALTH AND SCHOOL
READINESS IN EARLY CHILDHOOD

This material is based upon work supported by the Corporation for National and Community Service (CNCS) under Grant No. 11SIHMI001. Opinions or points of view expressed in this document are those of the authors and do not necessarily reflect the official position of, or a position that is endorsed by, CNCS or the CNCS's Social Innovation Fund. The Social Innovation Fund is a program of the CNCS, a federal agency that engages more than 5 million Americans in service through its AmeriCorps, Senior Corps, Social Innovation Fund, and Volunteer Generation Fund programs, and leads the President's national call to service initiative, United We Serve. Learn more at nationalservice.gov/Innovation.

This book was created in partnership with United Way for Southeastern Michigan (UWSEM), which facilitated the CNCS grant in the Detroit area. Opinions or points of view expressed in this book are those of the authors and do not necessarily reflect the official position of UWSEM. Copyrighted UWSEM logos and texts are used with the organization's permission. All rights reserved.

Special thanks to the staff of Macomb Family Services, who provided photos used in this book.

Comic art by Rebecca Tallarigo.

www.RebeccaTallarigo.com

For more information and further discussion, visit

BibToBackpack.org

ISBN: 978-1-942011-57-6

Version 1.0

Cover art and design by Rick Nease

www.RickNeaseArt.com

Publishing services provided by Front Edge Publishing, LLC

For information about customized editions, bulk purchases or permissions, contact Front Edge Publishing, LLC at info@FrontEdgePublishing.com

Contents

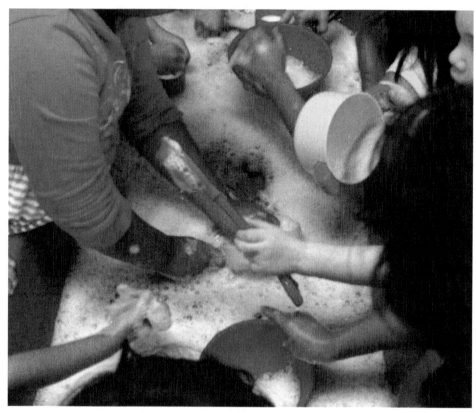

Many hands share the sudsy fun at a Play and Learn group.

"When we bring our energies together, they are increased a thousandfold. The whole can be much, much greater than the sum of its parts."

Thich Nhat Hanh, The Art of Communicating

This book is dedicated to the families and the community partners who join us in creating a lasting impact in the lives of young children.

A barn raising in Indiana in 1900.

Preface

From Dr. Wayne Baker

For centuries, barn raisings were a common experience across America. They still take place in some communities—particularly among the Amish—either to help a young family get started or after tornadoes or fires have swept across the landscape. Millions of Americans, today, have picked up a hammer for what may be the modern equivalent: Habitat for Humanity.

Think about everything that happens when a barn is raised or a Habitat home is built. It's a classic example of generalized reciprocity, or what many people refer to as "paying it forward." The community turns out en masse to help the family whose barn or home is being raised. That family—the one that will eventually own what is being built—most likely has helped with other similar building projects; in fact, the community probably wouldn't turn out if that family wasn't active. But beyond the wood and nails and the final structure, what the community really builds is a powerful sense of gratitude and an atmosphere of positive emotions. If a family wants a new barn or home, its members could contract with a professional construction crew—but involving the whole community builds something much larger than the final structure.

Christine Zimmerman, director of early childhood programming at Macomb Family Services, believes in and practices generalized reciprocity. That's one of two forms of reciprocity. First, there is direct reciprocity: I help you; you help me. That's an ethical and appropriate arrangement. But the other form of reciprocity is indirect: I help you; you feel grateful; you pay it forward and help another person.

In this book, Macomb Family Services CEO, Owen Pfaendtner, says, "We're not wallflowers; we volunteer. And we don't volunteer because we can see a specific payoff for each project or effort we make. Usually, there isn't a known payoff when we start working together. Rather, we bring our passion and we become actively involved because the whole community is better off when everyone contributes."

That's a classic summary of generalized reciprocity. We do expect some payoff, somewhere in the future: we believe that the community is going to be a better place—a place where people help one another using an indirect form of reciprocity. I give help freely and I ask for help freely. We give; we take. The community is better for it.

There are at least four benefits to what Owen, Christine and Macomb Family Services are doing in taking this approach to their work. The first three are common-sense benefits, if you think carefully about what happens in generalized reciprocity:

1. Relationships: You can't create real relationships in a single meeting and you can't hope to build relationships if the professionals you're working with are constantly shuffling. This group has found that, if the attendees at regional gatherings keep changing all the time, you're not going to build solid relationships. What creates a strong relationship? Repeated interactions with the same people over time—and that's what Christine is setting as her program's goal.

2. Endogenous resources: This term refers to the resources that are already right there in your team or your community; resources derived internally. You find them, identify them, energize them and generate use of them, but those resources really were there all along. That's a powerful way to increase your resources from the inside out.

3. Bigger payoffs: Generalized reciprocity means that payoffs are indirect. You can't always predict them or see them clearly; they take time, and may be long-term. But when they do come, they're better payoffs overall.

4. The fourth benefit is "Abundance mentality": Building a new mentality based on and relating to internal resourcefulness. Lots of organizations approach each new situation from a deficit mentality. People start saying: "We're being asked to do more with less!" And: "We don't have the resources to get our jobs done!" And, then: "If only we had more money, then we could do what needs to be done." If that's a common way of talking in your organization, than you may be operating under this kind of scarcity mentality. It leads to a focus on short-term transactions and immediate outcomes. Team members of this mentality are consistently focused on, "What's in it for me?"

But the kind of generalized reciprocity that Owen describes is based on an abundance mentality that assumes resources are present somewhere within the larger circle of the community. In this mentality, you begin to trust that the resources are there; they need only to be found and brought forward.

The long-term benefit of abundance mentality is that everyone in the organization is looking for resources in new ways. Team members begin to share the assumption that they're building social capital now, and that down the road, this will help all of them.

What Macomb Family Services is saying, really, is: Sure, it's possible to hire a construction company to build our barn; but we're all better off in the long run if we build this barn together.

__Wayne Baker__ is a sociologist on the senior faculty of the University of Michigan Ross School of Business and chief scientist with Give and Take, Inc., developer of the Give and Get app. Wayne works closely with his wife, Cheryl Baker, founder and CEO of Humax Corporation and Give and Take, Inc. For almost 20 years, he has provided tools such as the Reciprocity Ring® to enable groups around the world to engage in the practice of generalized reciprocity.

Welcome!

From Owen Pfaendtner and Christine Zimmerman

Some of the new research we are seeing on the importance of early childhood education is absolutely startling. You may have noticed the headlines of these striking studies yourself. One study that was especially troubling came from a team of experts planning for future prison construction. That's because one factor they were considering—when predicting prison expansion—was the number of children, nationwide, who would be unable to read by the third grade. If that seems baffling to you, then read this book and others in this series about a wide range of programs to address the urgent needs in early childhood education across Southeast Michigan. If children can't read by the third grade, the system begins to shuffle them along in many cases. Perhaps these children might find the help they need from a particularly supportive caregiver or teacher—but, if these children continue to lag behind in reading and writing, then that becomes a predictor of all kinds of problems that will emerge later in childhood, adolescence and adulthood.

Don't take our word for it. "The First Eight Years," a report from the Annie E. Casey Foundation, reads:

> From the moment they are born, young children are ready to learn. Behind a toddler's soft features and halting first steps, an unseen, but extremely high-stakes, activity is taking place—the building of a brain. What happens to children during those critical first years will determine whether their maturing brain has a sturdy foundation or a fragile one. …
>
> As a nation, we do not invest enough in our children's early years. In fact, federal spending on children is lowest when they are young, even though most brain

development occurs during this period. Worse, since 2010, federal spending on children has declined and is projected to continue to decline as a percentage of GDP over the next decade to its lowest point since the Great Depression.

Research shows that every dollar invested in high-quality early childhood education produces a 7 to 10 percent annual return on investment. As Nobel Prize-winning economist James Heckman points out, the longer society waits to intervene in children's lives, the more costly and difficult it becomes to make up for early setbacks—both for the struggling child and for the nation as a whole.

While intellectual development is critical to school readiness, it's only one of the developmental domains that predicts success in school. Over the past two decades, study after study has shown that all of the domains—and especially social-emotional development—are crucial to school performance and long-term success in life. Just prior to the publication of this book, the 2016 Annie E. Casey Foundation "KIDS COUNT" report stressed this point when comparing advantaged and disadvantaged communities:

Advantages that start at birth continue to accumulate as kids grow up. By the time children enter kindergarten, the children of higher-income, college-educated parents already have an enormous head start over kids from less advantaged families. Their cognitive and social-emotional skills are often far more developed, and their vocabularies are more extensive.

Children who live in nurturing families and are part of supportive communities have better social-emotional and learning outcomes. Parents struggling with financial hardship are more prone to stress and depression, which can interfere with effective parenting. These findings underscore the importance of two-generation strategies that strengthen families.

When communities have strong institutions and the resources to provide safety, good schools and quality support services, families and their children are more likely to thrive.

In Michigan, we share a statewide initiative best known by the term, "Great Start." This initiative was formed more than a decade ago to encourage a coordinated system of community resources and supports that provides a "great start" to children from birth to 5. The effort encourages regional school districts and nonprofits to collaborate on the kinds of services we provide to close the gaps in early education found across our state. This Great Start collaboration forms the architecture around the program you will read about in this book, as well as in Leaps & Bounds Family Services, an agency you will read about in another book in this series. Both agencies are connected in this collaboration through the Macomb Intermediate School District. Our professionals work mainly in Macomb County, an area just north of Detroit. However, in keeping with our commitment to regional cooperation, our teams also work and consult in areas outside of our county's boundaries. In reading this book, you will discover that paying close attention to relationships among professionals and between agencies is a key to our success. For example, our expansion in recent years was due to our work with partners at the Macomb Intermediate School District, United Way for Southeastern Michigan and the Corporation for National and Community Service's Social Innovation Fund.

Macomb County has really latched onto this commitment to collaboration. If you explore these programs across our state, you will find counties with dramatically different approaches to dealing with this age group. Collaboration and the freedom to work in different ways means that we do not try to compete with one another in serving particular needs or specific populations of families. It also means that, when new needs are identified in the community, we actively seek ways to address them. We help one another.

As the complexities of family life emerge and change throughout the years, we continue to discover new realities to which we must respond. Perhaps that is the case in your part of the country as well. In these pages you will learn about a team of professionals through our nonprofit agency, Macomb Family Services, that is working on a particularly challenging series of issues that can arise with children in daycare, in preschool and even at home. Our team also provides training for caregivers, teachers and parents. In these stories, you may be surprised by some of the problems we encounter—and some of the solutions we offer—as we work closely with the individuals who maintain our commitment to collaboration as we determine the next steps.

The challenges in childhood social-emotional development will grow in the years ahead. Within our state of Michigan, census projections suggest that increasing populations of young children will be in lower-income families and among larger numbers of immigrants whose primary language is not English. In our state, the national trend is mirrored: Fewer resources in education and in early learning are projected. It is imperative that services to ensure kindergarten readiness are strong.

Our team at Macomb Family Services hopes that this book will inspire you to recognize that collaboration is an important value; that healthy relationships lie at the core of all the best work we are doing; and that addressing what may seem like frustrating problems in early childhood can often lead to remarkably positive outcomes.

We hope that you find ideas in these pages that you can use.

We welcome you to read our story!

Owen Pfaendtner *is the CEO at Macomb Family Services and* **Christine Zimmerman** *is the director of early childhood programming at Macomb Family Services.*

Social Emotional START

* Intake and DECA form completed

1st Visit

* Observation

2nd Visit

* Further Observation
* Determine other needed assessments

3rd Visit

* Create a goal plan

4th Visit

* Reflection on strategies
* Ongoing observation to support goal implementation

Note: The Devereux Early Childhood Assessment (DECA) is a standardized questionnaire that helps evaluate many issues in a child's development and behavior.

Consult Timeline

5th Visit

* Reflection on strategies
* Outside referrals as needed

6th Visit

* Reflection on strategies
* Follow up on referrals

7th Visit

* Reflection on strategies
* Follow up on referrals
(Post DECA)

8th Visit

* Reflection on strategies going forward
* Reflection on Post DECA results
* Follow up on referrals

FINISH

Our Story

"Help!"

That word echoes every week at Macomb Family Services, in calls and emails that are requesting our services. Here are just a few of the recent messages that we received from parents, teachers and child care providers:

- "The biting has to stop. We've tried to work on this for a month, but the boy still can't control this. Something sets him off and he starts biting. Can you help us fix this?"

- "I've got a child in class who won't stop running around and hitting other children. The parents are at a loss—they don't see this behavior at home. We've tried everything we can think of in the classroom and nothing seems to work. You've worked with us before. We know what you can do in situations like this. We need your help again."

- "She doesn't respond to directions like the other children do. Instead, she just winds up acting very silly. She'll roll around the floor in the middle of the room. It's too disruptive for the other children. We need help."

- "She's extremely withdrawn. We keep finding her in the corner of the room. We need to respond to her more effectively. We need your fresh eyes on this."

- "Once a day, he just explodes and screams. Then, yesterday, he picked up a chair and threw it."

- "I'm a good teacher, but after two months of this, I'm thinking of quitting."

- "Can we get you to do a consultation with the whole class? Last year, when you did this, those weeks were a turning point for the class. Can you help us again?"

When a social emotional consultant is called to help, we have eight visits to make a difference. Take a look at the accompanying chart to see the typical focus of those eight visits. With years of experience, our consultants—Bronwyn Johnston and Alejandra Medina—know how to effectively use each of those visits to work toward a successful outcome.

The first step begins when the guardian completes the enrollment packet, which includes an enrollment form, consent form, and Devereux Early Childhood Assessment (DECA). The DECA is a strength based researched tool used as a social emotional assessment and planning system. The purpose is to promote resilience in young children. According to the Michigan Great Start Systems Team, children who are social emotionally healthy can

- Form close relationships with other people
- Express and manage emotions
- Explore new environments

Research has shown that children who have these skills are better able to pay attention, follow directions and persist in solving problems. All these are skills needed for future academic success. They support children in creating healthy relationships and in bouncing back from life's disappointments.

During this initial process, open-ended questions, observation and coaching techniques are used to begin building relationships and evaluate what is happening with the child and their caregivers. It can be scary for a family or teacher to allow a clinician into their life. They often wonder if they will be judged as a parent or as a teacher. Showing interest and care for them by remembering small details from the initial conversation, such as the name of their pet, goes a long way toward building trust. Whether we are sitting at a kitchen table, on a couch, or in a toddler chair in the classroom, our goal becomes helping caregivers understand their child's behavior and the positive ways in which we can address it. Having licensed clinicians is important to the work because there is a need to draw knowledge from a wide range of research and training, including basic child development, developmental disorders, trauma informed practice, neurobiology, family systems, ecological systems and early childhood mental health. As we develop in relationship and understanding with the family, we are helping them form a clear vision of how they want their family to work. Sometimes, we are helping a child feel safe, and sometimes we are trying to get a child to sleep in their own bed.

By the third visit we are creating a goal plan that captures the vision of what the parent or teacher hopes for the child. Our role as consultants for future visits becomes helping families problem solve how to get there. The secret is, we don't primarily work with the children, we work with caregivers to support them. Consultants intervene through coaching a parent or modeling in the presence of a caregiver so that they can re-create it and continue the success.

Bronwyn Johnston, one of our consultants, remembers one grandmother who requested a series of home visits to help with some of her grandchild's troubling behavior. Bronwyn made two initial visits to assess the child and family needs. The child was having frequent aggressive outbursts of screaming, biting, and hitting when he was angry. Through assessment Bronwyn realized that his grandmother did not understand child development and what she could expect from the child. It became clear to Bronwyn that discipline was used as a punishment rather than consequences as an opportunity to learn. The third time Bronwyn knocked on that family's door, the grandmother showed her into the living room and they sat down to talk about some of the strategies for addressing these behaviors.

After a few minutes, the grandmother held up her hand as if to pause the conversation for a moment and asked Bronwyn "Do you feel like you are here more to work with me?"

"Yes," Bronwyn smiled, and nodded. "That's right."

The program director, Christine Zimmerman, reinforces this approach in many ways. Our consultants are not assigned to intervene, make an expert assessment and then deliver instructions like a medical doctor, who might declare a diagnosis and order a treatment plan; rather, these consultants are observing adult-child interactions and using a strength-based process to identify key assets the child has, in addition to any problems or deficits that may be identified in their visits. The child's own strengths often become the key to working through the challenges. In this way, the consultants forge cooperative relationships with parents, teachers and child care providers—as well as the children—to share ideas and cooperatively work out solutions.

As you continue to read this book, you will hear stories and learn more about the strategy phases of the process as outlined on the timeline.

The fourth through the seventh visits are where the real change begins. During this phase the consultant supports the caregiver in reflecting on their experience with the strategies and notice changes in the child. Reflection helps caregivers determine why a child's behavior is occurring and in what ways they can meet the child's needs. When the consultant notices additional concerns, such as a developmental delays or sensory processing challenges, families are connected to appropriate resources.

Western society tends to focus on a "quick fix." The temptation is to see a behavior and "prescribe" a strategy. Our consultants believe in the value of reflective practice as a way to more deeply assess and impact change. Take a family in which a three year old cries uncontrollably for hours when separated from his mom. His mom couldn't run to Target because she would be called home due to the hysterical tears. When dad tried to help with any daily routines, such as dressing or getting him in the car, he would tell dad to leave and push him away. Dad's work schedule meant that he was often away, sometimes for weeks at a time. Through reflective conversation, mom came to the realization that her responses of stepping in when dad was caring for him was essentially telling the child that his dad wasn't a competent caregiver. After coming to this realization, mom was able to adjust her own responses in a way that made the child feel safe in the care of others. Dad was happy to enjoy a better relationship with his son and participate in his care.

The last visit or two are spent ensuring the family has the tools to continue being successful. This may include new strategies, reviewing strategies, or following up on referrals. Caregivers are asked to complete a follow up DECA that gives them a visual on improvements that have been made in the child's social emotional development. Time is spent reflecting on these changes and steps for the future.

Reflective supervision is an essential component throughout the consultants' work. This is a parallel process that supports consultants in their reflection of the work with families and caregivers. Reflection allows a safe space for vulnerability and exploration to learn and discover together. This allows the consultant to expand their thinking and see from various perspectives. It isn't about needing to be an "expert," it's about supporting new ways of thinking. This is the same process consultants engage in with the caregivers and that the caregivers begin to engage in with their child.

From Alejandra Medina, a social-emotional consultant at Macomb Family Services

In addition to consulting in homes and classrooms, I also organize six-week workshops to help parents with many of the challenges they face in raising young children. In each of the sessions, we meet for two hours and, each time, I bring helpful material with me to share with the group. But the most important activity in these classes is the discussion that involves all of the parents who attend.

Just as we do in our individual consultations, our classes use a strength-based process. That means: I don't allow the whole session to focus on negative behavior. We focus on the strengths we can find in our children, and in ourselves, to understand what is happening—and to respond in new ways. It is important to reassure parents that their children—whatever problems they may be experiencing at the moment—certainly are not little demons. Of course parents love their children! But after months of living with some of these troubling behaviors, parents can fall into a habit of blaming themselves for problems that they just can't seem to fix. They can start to feel helpless, as if this behavior is some kind of demon they just can't tame.

We are helping parents to refocus their viewpoints on these situations—to change their understanding of what is happening. Even if their children are expressing themselves in an angry or violent way, this almost always is because these children are trying hard to express something to the people around them. It's frustrating when children want to take part in activities and express themselves but, for some reason, find themselves unable to do this effectively. This behavior can cause serious problems. If it happens in a classroom, it can be very frustrating. Parents can start thinking that they've failed; that they're bad parents. We offer these classes to help parents move away from feelings of blame and shame that can so easily result from these situations. We're giving them new information and they're seeing their children in a new light.

A good discussion among parents, focused in the right way, can be a very rich experience for everyone in the circle. Each parent gets to share; they all learn; and they develop relationships with other parents—a very important source of reassurance and insight. They get excited about new possibilities with their children. And, in every class I lead, the parents leave with something to try at home—some type of homework that will help them. They practice what we discussed in the class and, when we come back for the next session, we talk about how it worked out for them. Parents like coming back to a group like this. They usually see relationships improving at home. They are renewed and refreshed, and often, they walk away with new, supportive friends they can contact in the future.

That's our approach in these classes: to bring our outside expertise into a discussion with parents and teachers and to focus on the strengths we all can utilize to make things better. We are changing the way these parents look at both their situation and the resources around them.

We are offering new pairs of glasses. If we do our work effectively, everyone begins to see the world in a new way.

From Bronwyn Johnston, a social-emotional consultant at Macomb Family Services

The work we do in leading classes or workshops is very important. So are the eight-week consultations that we conduct in schools and home settings to help with the behavioral problems that are referred to us. That work really is awesome, when we see some of the results that we're able to achieve.

One of the biggest strengths of our program is that we're not just limited to consultations in classrooms or to the workshops that we teach; we also spend a lot of time in individual home visits. It was during a series of home visits that I encountered the mom who, in that third session, suddenly realized that our work was as much about her as it was about her son.

Our work usually involves an entire circle of relationships. It's that bigger picture that is so easily missed by busy parents—especially moms who may feel overwhelmed or isolated with their small children. A call for help is often our starting point if a parent is reaching out to us. Perhaps we get the request in an email or someone telephones us to make that initial connection. At that point, parents are usually frustrated. They're anxious. They're struggling. Of course they love their children. They love their kids so much that they're starting to worry that this problem may be their fault. I've actually had moms tell me things like: "I guess I must be the worst parent on the planet." Of course that's not true, but they're beginning to feel that way.

Then, if a connection is made, we are able to make our eight visits. We can't fix everything in the world in eight visits, but usually parents wind up feeling empowered in ways they may never have expected.

"Nice to Meet You!"

While parents and teachers are a central focus of our work, in the end, it's all about the kids. We work toward ensuring that children enter school ready to learn; that parents have the tools and resources to support their children's education; and that communities and schools also support young children's learning, growth and development. Usually, for our team, that involves spotting emerging problems, responding with help from everyone involved in the situation—and, sometimes, connecting with other programs through referrals.

In the spring of 2016, as we were preparing this book, we visited one of the Play and Learn groups that comprise a major component of our program. These very popular groups offer hands-on early learning opportunities for both children and parents. Through Play and Learn, we invite children and adults to practice a wide range of skills that are essential for success in preschool and eventually in kindergarten. These groups also are opportunities for observation and referrals when staff members spot problematic behavior or developmental issues that should be addressed beyond the Play and Learn program.

We arrived at a Play and Learn site—an elementary school in an ethnically diverse neighborhood—and found a big room with colorful carpeting and posters on the wall. The first two arrivals that morning were a 4-year-old boy and his grandmother. The facilitator, La Don Williams, was just starting to unpack the materials that eventually would spread across a half-dozen round tables. All the furniture was set at a height that was perfect for the preschoolers who soon would be swarming into the space with their parents (nearly all mothers) on this particular morning.

This boy's grandmother noticed a bookshelf near their table and asked, "Want to read a book?"

The boy nodded enthusiastically, and his little hand shot toward one particular picture book, which he flipped open and placed between them on the table.

"What are you reading?" asked one of our representatives, as a couple of Macomb Family Services team members settled into chairs on the other side of the table.

The little boy simply pointed to the book—an obvious answer to the question.

"What's that book about?"

"Dinosaurs," he said.

"Oh, he loves dinosaurs!" his grandmother added. "We just took him to see that dinosaur movie."

The boy grinned broadly. "I love that dinosaur movie!"

"What's your favorite kind of dinosaur?" we inquired.

"Blue ones," he said, then added, "And green." A pause. "But I like blue ones best."

"Blue dinosaurs?"

The boy quickly flipped through the book until he found a double-page illustration of an enormous blue creature. "Like this one! See? It's blue!"

It sure was! Bright blue, in fact. "Are you in school?" one of our facilitators asked.

"I'm in preschool," he said proudly. We began talking about his favorite activities in preschool, but just then, two other children rushed to the table and the whole conversation shifted to a story about a pet dog doing something hilarious that morning. The boy's attention soon was drawn toward interacting with the other kids, who had become his friends through this group.

When the Play and Learn session was well underway, we noticed this same grandmother and her grandson making brightly colored art. As is usually the case at Play and Learn, they were both seated at the table, using scissors, glue, string and other materials from of a big pile of art supplies. The boy had sorted through this array to create his own work of art.

"Can you show us what you've made?" one of our team members asked.

He launched into a description of the colors he had chosen and of the way he had added various pieces.

"And where will this go when you get home?"

"We'll hang it in my room," he said.

As we stood up to move on and talk with other families, the boy waved and politely said, "Nice to meet you!"

What we did not know until after that morning session had ended—and we were able to debrief with La Don Williams—is that this little boy, until very recently, had been silent at Play and Learn.

"You had two whole conversations with him?" La Don asked. "Tell me what he said."

We played some of the audio we had recorded and described the conversations. "Amazing!" La Don said. "Whole sentences. So clear. And polite, too! I love that: 'Nice to meet you!'"

We learned that the boy had had problems enunciating words. Even his parents and grandparents could not understand much of what he was trying to express, although they got along well enough that the boy was still growing up a bright and happy child in other ways. However, when he started at Play and Learn in the fall of 2015, he was suddenly interacting with strangers. His lack of verbal clarity prevented other children from making sense of what he was trying to express. The other kids weren't mean, La Don explained; they just lost interest in trying to understand him and moved on to other activities among the lively array of tables and crafts. It was simply far easier to talk with other children. Soon, the boy found himself isolated and he stopped even trying to speak.

"But his parents and his grandmother are very involved. We helped them with referrals and then they must have followed through on those referrals, because they clearly got him the help he needed," La Don said. That's exactly what happened, we later learned, when talking with the family. They had begun working with a speech therapist and participating in other supplemental programs they had discovered through connections made through the Play and Learn group. That little boy was on the verge of isolation, self-imposed silence and a frustrating start to school. Instead, he is now on a pathway toward a bright future, say the professionals working with the boy and his family.

"Amazing," La Don said, shaking her head. "See? There's a whole lot more than you may realize happening in these Play and Learn groups."

As she finished picking up the supplies, she smiled again. "How far that boy has come!" And she turned to us. "I like that. 'Nice to meet you!'"

How We Got Started

From Owen Pfaendtner, CEO of Macomb Family Services

Today, Macomb Family Services provides a wide range of family-related counseling services and other programs, as well as homes for adults with developmental disabilities. We currently serve residents of Macomb County and surrounding communities, but we started as a very small nonprofit in 1957. At that time, a whole wave of grassroots organizations were forming across the country with the intent of bringing mental health services into communities. Our nonprofit was started by a group of families in Mount Clemens originally called the Children's Aid and Family Services organization. From the beginning, they received funds from what is today United Way for Southeastern Michigan. Our work with United Way has been a great partnership throughout all of these years.

Our mission always has been to respond to the needs that we see emerging in our communities—and that means we've tried to change, adapt to and fill the emerging gaps with our services. Our mission has been "to enhance the health and well-being of others, and promote social and personal change." But we're always looking for needs that pop up; then, we try to secure funding to meet those needs. And we're always trying to ensure that needs are met, especially in communities that often are underserved by other programs. For example, in the 1980s—as awareness of domestic violence became more widespread—we were one of the nonprofits that responded. To this day, we still have a program that responds to that challenge. We follow the evidence of what is working. Over the years, we have developed a number of programs, and then we've carefully evaluated what is working and what is not. As a result, we continue to specialize in the areas where we're really making a difference.

One of our most effective programs is a series of trainings that we provide for teachers and child care providers. Over the years, Christine Zimmerman and her team have presented more than 30 different kinds of training. As we do that, we continue to ask ourselves: How do we get better at this whole process? The mission has always been clear: We're helping children become more socially and emotionally functional by the time they reach kindergarten. But the recipe for reaching that goal continues to evolve.

We value collaboration. The story of the little boy who had trouble enunciating—then began to feel isolated and wouldn't speak for a while in his Play and Learn group—is a perfect example of our collaborative approach. La Don realized that there was an issue at hand and she made referrals. We couldn't do everything necessary to help that boy improve his speech, but we knew professionals who could. That's why we make a point of learning as much as we can about all of the other services available to families in our area. When we spot an issue like the one this little boy was facing, we can wind up helping his family even more— through referrals for lots of additional services. If we're having difficulty figuring out how to respond to a particular case, we call around to expand on our network of contacts. We regularly participate in regional organizations—and we do this in many ways. For example, we participate in community open houses where we can make contact with parents while we're also learning about other agencies and nonprofits participating in the open house.

It's important to understand our approach to these regional gatherings. We don't just show up at events and sit there—just showing up is short of the mark we set for ourselves. If we've chosen to participate, than we truly engage in the work and show our passion for it. We're not wallflowers; we volunteer. And we don't do this because we can see a specific payoff for each project or effort we make. Usually, there isn't a known payoff when we start working together. We bring our passion and we become actively involved because the whole community is better off when everyone contributes.

Wayne Baker, from the University of Michigan, calls this "generalized reciprocity"—and that's a good way to describe this value we share. Sometimes we may participate in 10 gatherings or meetings before we discover some little gem that pops to the surface—some idea, or collaboration, or fresh insight that tells us: Yeah, this effort is well worth it.

If you are engaged in this kind of work, you have to realize that the models for best practices are continually changing. We can respond to those changes most effectively if we have a solid network of relationships all across the community that can help us to continue to evolve in how we respond to families' needs.

Collaboration is Crucial

From Lisa Sturges, the Early Learning Communities program manager for United Way for Southeastern Michigan. Lisa previously played a key role in the Macomb Intermediate School District's coordination of these programs

Today, United Way's commitment to Early Learning Communities (ELC) has the goal of working with families and caregivers to ensure that they have the resources they need to get children ready for school. We want parents to be able to find these resources wherever they live in this part of Michigan, whether they're in Wayne, Oakland or Macomb County. Our ELC programs are funded in various ways. Some are funded through the Social Innovation Fund (SIF), like the SIF-funded portions of Macomb Family Services and Leaps & Bounds.

Before moving into my current role, I was the Great Start Collaborative coordinator for the Macomb Intermediate School District. In Michigan, there is a collaborative program in every county whose goal is fostering programs that will help families with children from birth to age 5, so that children are ready when they start school. Together, coordinators of these programs look at what services are already available and try to identify gaps in the services or in the geographic area where they are provided. If a gap is found, it's asked: Who might support an expansion here? There are other states across the U.S. that have systems in place like this, too. Over the years, coordinators of these collaborative programs have appreciated learning from some of the work done in other states, and now, community leaders across the country are able to learn from their work.

Here in Michigan, a collaborative approach started nearly a decade ago, in about a dozen counties. Macomb County is currently in the second phase of expanding this effort statewide. Generally, collaboration has five broad areas of concern that relate to the well-being of children and their families. To have a great start in school, families need to ensure that their children have physical health; social-emotional health; early child care and education; and parental leadership and support. From what I have seen nationally, Michigan is distinctive in focusing on the entire range of early childhood, from 0 to 5, while emphasizing parent leadership in the process.

When the Social Innovation Fund grant became available, this naturally was something that our collaborative wanted to make available to the agencies in our region. We were always trying to cross boundaries to ensure the broadest coverage of services, so it was natural for the Macomb Intermediate School District to work with Macomb Family Services and Leaps & Bounds to partner on funding through SIF.

As the Macomb regional partnership developed, the school district helped to organize the partners, manage data and evaluation, coordinate some of the screening and help to facilitate Play and Learn groups and home visits. Its signature project through the SIF initiative has been the Kindergarten Readiness Camps. The camps were designed to help pre-kindergarten students transition into kindergarten with success. The focus was to help children build foundational literacy skills in an engaging and developmentally appropriate way. Leaps & Bounds Family Services' SIF-funded initiatives include the establishment of Parent Resource Rooms in three school districts within Macomb and Wayne Counties, the implementation of Parent and Child Interactive Learning through play groups and a series of home visits focused on educational development using the Parents as Teachers curriculum. Macomb Family Services focuses on the social-emotional development of young children through parent workshops, consultations, training for teachers and caregivers and Play and Learn groups. Together, we present a much wider range of services than any one group could hope to offer.

Our goal is to strengthen the resources available for families by combining our efforts—and that's what we were able to achieve. If we do our work effectively, we build strong relationships through a culture in which we stress that this is "our" work—not just "my work." It's "our" responsibility, together—not just "their" responsibility. I am not saying that we have fixed everything in Southeast Michigan. We have high rates of poverty in many of our communities. Like other parts of the U.S., we face diminishing financial resources and, thus, smaller budgets. But through this collaboration we encourage cooperation on the best ideas and practices rather than fighting over the available money from separate camps that may wind up creating more gaps than are filled.

In my experience with the two Macomb nonprofits that collaborated with the school district in the SIF grant, I think it sends a powerful message about the distinctive character of the leaders at Macomb Family Services and Leaps & Bounds. These leaders are willing to come together regionally, lay everything they're doing on the table and see how their efforts fit with what others are doing. Not every agency is willing to work so cooperatively. It takes trust. It takes confidence in the abilities of your team. And, in the end, it's that kind of open sharing that's the basis for a solid working relationship in helping families—and that's why we do this work every day.

Training: The Value of Learning Together

At Macomb Family Services, we provide many forms of training for parents, teachers and child care providers. In developing our classes, we draw on research-based materials whenever possible. High quality early childhood development classes are offered to support teachers and parents in building skills needed to support children's learning and growth. Participants in these engaging classes have opportunities to learn new ideas and reflect with each other. Another form of training is through a free, six-week workshop for parents that was developed at Vanderbilt University's Center on the Social and Emotional Foundations for Early Learning. We call our series the Positive Parenting Workshop, and in it, we focus on understanding social-emotional development; appropriate expectations; responding to challenging behavior; and promoting resiliency in children. The goal is to help parents understand why their children do what they do and to enhance parent-child relationships. In addition, we make adaptations to educational materials for our particular communities and we have also developed some of our own curricula.

When our work is successful, parents feel so empowered that they wind up forming their own networks with other parents. When we began this work, we often had to wait for opportunities to hold classes. Now, we get many referrals from past participants. A couple of moms have even discovered a vocation in working with children. One example is a mother who had two preschool-aged children when our Macomb Family Services team first met her. She had heard about our Macomb Family Services child-development classes and wound up attending several of them. She told us that the classes were a revelation.

The first thing she realized was: "I had spent a lot of money on toys and saw that my older daughter didn't play with them! I realized it's not about the fancy, colorful toys." In our Macomb Family Services training, we emphasize that children love to play simple games and with things that are often already in the home.

"I started respecting my children and letting them explore things like playing in the water, peeling eggs and helping to make dough," the mother told us. "I started math concepts with my daughter without her even realizing that she was learning. We would work on shapes through different objects in our house. We would use math concepts like: How tall is your castle?

The impact is more than words can express! This is our style of thinking now."

When this mother began taking classes, her older daughter was 4, but the little girl was having a difficult time adjusting to child care. Learning to get used to a separation from Mom during those classes in the safe environment we provide at child care—with mom in a nearby room—was an important step in helping this girl become emotionally ready for a daily program. When she eventually was enrolled in preschool, she was able to make a smooth transition.

"Now I know what is developmentally appropriate for my girls," she said, explaining her new sense of confidence and her growing awareness of early learning. "Now, we enjoy activities such as reading, pretend play and exploring flowers."

A year after she began taking classes, this mother took the first steps toward establishing a child care center in her home. Her planning was shaped by the knowledge and experience she gained through Macomb Family Services. "I feel comfortable starting this new work because I know I can call upon the mentors I have at Macomb Family Services if I have questions or need support."

From Debbie Giddey, a Great Start Readiness Program (GSRP) lead teacher at a center in Warren, Michigan

I have both a bachelor's and a master's degree in early childhood education, but I am a big believer in taking every training opportunity that's available to me—which is how I first encountered Macomb Family Services. I initially had Bronwyn Johnston come into my classroom for a consultation, and since then, I've been involved in many of the Macomb Family Services programs. My only wish is that they'd been offering all of these programs years ago.

I first connected with Macomb Family Services when I was teaching at another facility. I had a little girl in my classroom whose behavior was very challenging: she was 4 years old and she just would not sit still. She would interrupt me all the time. And she would get up and move around like she was flying through my classroom, with her arms out like wings. I'm a trained teacher, but I needed some help with this. I needed fresh ideas about how to respond.

That's when my director at the time told me about Macomb Family Services trainings, and gave me a flier about their classes. I saw one class on behavior challenges among preschoolers, and I immediately signed up for it. When I attended, I got some great ideas.

It turns out that this little girl needed special attention. One thing she needed was a feeling of being grounded in the room. It's as if her sense of gravity wasn't fully developed and she wasn't sure about the way her body was moving around our room—so she stuck out her arms to balance herself and zoomed around. It was her way of coping with the sensation of move-ment. I learned that one way to respond to that kind of situation is to provide the child with a heavy stuffed animal to carry around. She loved it! She held onto it and it helped her to stop flying around my classroom. I also learned that she needed a lit-tle more of my time. Some of the ideas they gave me were to embrace her occasionally, to give her a hug—and to pay a little more attention to her: find out what she wanted to do and how she was feeling. That kind of extra attention made a big differ-ence, too.

I was sold on that first class experience, so I signed up for more training right away. In fact, I think I signed up for a whole list of trainings that Macomb Family Services was offering.

As a classroom teacher myself, I can tell you: I get a lot of great ideas that I can use right away from this kind of train-ing. I'm a mom, as well. I have three kids, who now are aged 16 to 21. I didn't start college myself until my children were in school. My real passion has always been working with children 6 and younger. They're like sponges at that age. They absorb so much information from the world around them that I am eager to make sure that they have great opportunities to learn. It's so important at that age.

I earned both my bachelor's and master's degrees in this field, and I know that some people think that, once you gradu-ate, you should be all done with learning. But that's not the case if you want to remain effective. I've actually taken some of the Macomb Family Services classes more than once because each time, new ideas surface. It's part of their approach to teaching—they continually ask the participants to help them raise new questions and respond with fresh ideas. Plus, you meet other teachers and get to share ideas and challenges. You realize you're not alone.

The field of education is constantly changing. Researchers continue to identify new childhood behaviors and offer new responses. I love helping children to learn as much as they can, so I'm a big advocate of this Macomb Family Services style of training. When I think of that style, I think of La Don Williams, who has taught many of the classes I've taken. She doesn't just show up and run through the curriculum; she involves us as participants and wants to know what's going on in our classrooms. She's teaching with an eye to leaving each of us with something we can carry home and use right away. If we stump her with a question, she promises to get back with us—and she does.

Sometimes, the strength-based approach they take can be frustrating. More than once, I've wished I could just tell her about a problem and that she'd give me an answer: tell me what to do. But that's not how this works. She always asks lots of questions and then we work together from that point. She gives me lots of ideas, but more than that, she's always helping me to find a new perspective of my situation. I can tell that the people I've worked with from Macomb Family Services—La Don and Bronwyn—share my passion. That goes a long way to helping me remain excited about walking into my own classroom each day.

*From La Don Williams, an early childhood specialist
and parent educator who is also a supervisor at Macomb
Family Services' Early Learning Communities programs.
La Don still teaches classes and runs Play and Learn
groups, but the Macomb Family Services program
is expanding in 2016, so she also supervises other
professionals who do similar work*

We help parents and teachers realize that they're not alone. There are lots of other resources around us in this community—and early learning doesn't need to cost an arm and a leg for a lot of fancy, expensive supplies. I don't just talk about that. I show others what I mean.

Let's take a very common problem: The waning midday nap. As children get older, they stop wanting to take a midday nap. Biologically, this can happen at a range of ages; some children remain good sleepers for a long time. But when children are somewhere between the ages of 3 and 4, there's a tendency for them to lose a natural ability to fall asleep by themselves. The parents start having to encourage them to lie down. The closer the child is to age 4, the more likely he or she won't fall asleep, even if they are convinced to go to their room and lie down. Parents know about this: by age 4—or sometimes sooner—a check-in after 10 minutes will often reveal that the child is still awake. Their bodies just can't seem to shut down in a way that lets them take a nap. Almost always by the time a child is 4 and almost 5, this is a common situation.

Well, if you're a parent, you know that nap time serves many purposes! In classes, when I ask about this, many parents will say, "Hey, we can't give up nap time! I depend on nap time to get so many things done!" Or, "It's my break in the day, too, and I need it even if my child doesn't need it!" Of course, it's good for children, too, to make sure they get some downtime during the day. They need to relax.

So, when we begin sharing ideas in response to this situation, many parents find that there actually are a lot of things that they can try. One easy solution is to let the child take a favorite book to bed with them. Even if they can't fall asleep, reading or

La Don Williams demonstrates making a big sand timer using supplies many people may already have at home.

looking at pictures in a book is a quiet activity that helps them relax. Certain toys can make good companions for this down time, too. It depends on the child. But the question remains: How do we mark the time? How does the child know how long nap time will last?

One idea I demonstrate for the parents is this: Make a "sand timer"(or, in our case, I usually demonstrate making a "salt timer"). It might take a little trial and error, but you can make a simple timer either with some sand or with a container of Morton's salt—something many of us already have at home—and two empty water bottles, like the ones most of us recycle all the time. You have to be careful about how you make the hole between the two bottle caps, but with a little practice, you can make a timer that takes quite a while for the top bottle of sand or salt to empty into the bottom bottle. The timer I demonstrate just requires the use of a simple tool to make the hole in the two caps: you could use a drill, or just the sharp tip of a pair of scissors. Once the hole is made, I like to join the bottles with some pretty duck tape. If there's not enough sand or salt in the two-water-bottle model, I've also made timers with empty 2-liter pop bottles—and those timers take much longer to move all of their contents from the top bottle to the bottom one. My only caution on that version is this: Make sure the plastic bottles are clear so that the child can see the sand moving.

After my demonstration, some parents may decide not to make a timer. And that's OK, too. There are other options for marking time. Most of us have some kind of simple, very visible timer at home. See what you've got in your kitchen. Or go to a dollar store and you'll usually find simple timers. My idea is to give parents lots of ideas that don't cost much money.

Overall, this training stresses the many fairly easy, inexpensive ways that we can adapt family life to help children better develop. Most parents like that approach. Sometimes, though, we have to address parents who are really ill-equipped when dealing with their young children. For example, I once had a parent tell me, "My child has to fit into my world. I'm not going to try to fit my life into my child's world." What she meant was that she didn't want to adjust her own lifestyle to make room for her child. Well, we can't create win-win situations with an attitude like that. Young children require a lot of patience, and we *do* have to adjust to their development, which I can tell you does not fit into all adult lifestyles.

So, a lot of what I'm doing is helping parents begin to appreciate what is happening with their children—why children do what they do at different ages. I've just described a very common question: Why does my 3-year-old no longer want to take a nap? In this situation, we first help parents understand that this is a normal development. A child's body, at some point, no longer requires as much sleep. Then, with that understanding of the behavior, we move on to share ideas for responding to this change in the family.

From Bronwyn Johnston, a social-emotional consultant at Macomb Family Services

What La Don has just described illustrates why our approach is effective. When we start a workshop, we're not just standing up in front of a bunch of people and talking at them in a long lecture format. We do work from a solid curriculum, but the way we teach from that curriculum makes all the difference. Usually, our approach involves opening up the topic to a lot of discussion. It's not as effective to stand up and proclaim: "This is the problem!" Or, "This is how you should respond!" It's more effective to involve the parents in a discussion of what works for them and to let them compare stories with other parents, to see the range of behaviors they're experiencing—and to hear a whole range of responses. We know we're effectively running a workshop when we hear parents begin to say, "Hmmm, that's interesting, but have you tried it this other way?"

From Alejandra Medina, a social-emotional consultant at Macomb Family Services

We're all very passionate about these workshops, because we've seen the difference they can make if we fully involve the parents. We want to get them so involved that I sometimes describe it as "inviting the inner child to come out in the classroom."

While helping parents to understand the best ways to interact with their children, we find a lot of parents who simply haven't thought of doing things like getting right down on the floor with their children and participating as the children play. Many parents do that, of course, but it's difficult for some parents. Some parents never had this experience with their own parents when they were young. So it's a new idea for them. One thing I like to do in workshops is to actually get the parents down on the floor. We sit on the floor. We play on the floor. We call these "workshops" because this is a very experiential style of learning.

From Bronwyn Johnston

This "open" style of workshop encourages parents to become really invested in each other. They get to know one another and learn each other's daily struggles. Sometimes, when a new series begins, the parents may know one another: that's true if a particular group of parents decides to come together for one of our workshops. But I've also had a lot of groups in which no one knew anyone else when they first walked through the door. Often, parents who attend are responding to a flier we've posted in the community, so almost everyone is a stranger in that first session. When a workshop ends, some parents go their own way—but other parents keep in contact. Other times, the parents will continue to see each other because they may decide to attend a particular Play and Learn together. Sometimes, one successful class will spark another. We like to hear parents ask: "Can you do another workshop for us?" We have lots of topics that we can address in various kinds of workshops. There's a long list. We have the Positive Parenting series. We have individual trainings, too. Just a few examples of the topics we address are: outdoor activities with young children; reading with preschoolers; toddler conflict; children's sign language; and problem-solving. There's no shortage of helpful subject matter.

If you are reading this book and you plan to use some of our ideas for your own program, it is important to remember that our approach to relationships extends into all areas of our work. It shapes the way we organize our workshops; the way we work with teachers, caregivers and parents; and the way we cooperate with other members of our team. It begins with Christine Zimmerman's approach to interviewing potential employees. First, Christine's style of interviewing shows how much she values relationships. Then, she always asks questions such as, "Describe a time you had a conflict at work?" Or, "How did you contribute to the situation?" If someone is unable to talk about their conflict resolution while working with other people, or is unable to describe a contribution they made as a part of a team, then Christine isn't likely to hire that person. Our reputation in the communities we serve depends on this approach to relationships.

Now that we are more widely known, people will call us more than once—and they will refer others to us because they know that no matter who is able to respond from our agency, they'll be in good hands.

Classroom Consultation: What's Really Going On?

At Macomb Family Services we provide social-emotional consultation for children prior to the start kindergarten with the goal of preparing them for success when they enter school. The program assists parents and teachers in a variety of ways depending on the needs of the child and the parent or teacher. Children are assessed using the standardized Devereux Early Childhood Assessment (DECA), our own observation and other tools as needed. Our goal is to determine the strengths of and the support needed by the children we are serving through these short-term, intensive interventions. Our visits provide activities, modeling and insights for adults that will help promote self-regulation, social and emotional health and kindergarten readiness for the children. When more intensive evaluation is needed, or if a child is found to have intensive mental health needs, the clinicians work with the family to connect them with those particular support systems. The program promotes both teachers' and parents' understanding of children's behaviors, so that they can model, encourage and foster healthy behaviors. This process guides the children in their discovery of new and healthier skills that allow them to maintain richer interactions with their peers and the adults in their environment.

There are two ways our consultants are called into a classroom. One option is because of a single child whose behavior concerns the teacher. Another option for teachers who want to gain broader support for their students is a series of visits in which one of our consultants works with the entire class. In that option, we assess the class as a whole. In both cases the DECA is used both before and after our consulting series. The consultant then assesses the whole group using DECA and classroom observation. Activities are modeled in the class using material from the Center on the Social and Emotional Foundations for Early Learning and other resources, focused on the needs of the class. Reflective conversations occur with the teacher and consultant after each session. When there are children in the classroom with more intensive needs, then individual plans are created for those children. The purpose is to build the teacher's skills by supporting the class and by raising the social and emotional skills of the children.

It is important to remember when we are working with a classroom that building a strong relationship with the teacher will impact the greatest change. We consider some of the fears a teacher might have about a consultant working in the class. They may feel judged as a teacher, afraid they will fail, afraid we will say negative things to their director, or feel protective about their space. These fears all set the stage for a teacher who can appear defensive and closed even when they are seeking help.

Considering these fears, the way we approach teachers influences the direction of the relationship and the work together. When preparing to begin work with a teacher, the consultant asks the teacher about the best time of day for observation. The consultant talks about what the program encompasses and what commitment will be involved. We provide a picture of what the sessions will look like. The consultant explores the teachers concerns regarding social emotional development and the teacher may discuss concerns about specific children. When entering the classroom we ask what space would be the best place to observe so that we are not interfering with their day. In this way, teachers start off feeling that we are there to partner with them rather than to impose something on them.

Once the foundation is laid for relationship, consultants are able to effectively partner with the teacher to achieve results, which can be multifaceted. One result can be a sense of validation for the teacher who feels alone in their observations and is affirmed that someone outside their system is seeing the same concerns that the teacher has seen. Another possible result is that the teacher feels safe enough to open to other perspectives and see the child through a different lens.

Understanding the meaning behind the child's behaviors allows the teacher to communicate and partner with the parent to support the child. This is particularly helpful when other resources are needed. It also empowers the teacher to more effectively address the behaviors they are seeing and ultimately improves the child's relationships between their teacher and other children in the classroom. As these relationships are built, and the teacher sees the child in different ways, they are able to better support the child in their emotional development and academics leading to kindergarten readiness.

From Sandra Glovak, a registered, licensed occupational therapist (OTR/L) and the director of Sensory Systems Clinic in St. Clair Shores, Michigan. Sandra regularly consults with the Macomb Family Services team

I'm an expert in working with children who have mental health and sensory processing disorders: a range of conditions that includes attachment disturbances, anxiety disorders, feeding and eating problems, attention issues, aggression, depression and even autism. When I consult with the Macomb Family Services team, we go over their current cases and talk about ways to respond.

For example, if we encounter children who run a lot and who seem to have a challenge with gravity and their own body's movement, then one idea is to give the child a fairly heavy toy to carry. The toy might be something like a beanbag frog that weighs around four pounds. That particular issue is technically called "gravitational insecurity," which is an anxiety or fear of being upright and moving around. These young children just don't feel the pull of gravity on their bodies in the way most of us experience it. This insecurity can take many forms. I remember a case in which a mother reported that her child would begin screaming uncontrollably any time she put him into a shopping cart and began to move around a particular store. She'd have to leave the store because he just wouldn't stop. Eventually, we were able to determine that the problem was big ceiling fans in this particular store. The child would look up and began to fear that these big fans might suck him right up into the air, and he would be hurt. The mother had no idea what was happening, but together, we learned that fear of the fans was causing the behavior in the store. Now, that's an unusual and specific example. In most cases, children with this developmental issue become insecure and overly active, and the adults around them experience this as an unexplained problem that often involves a lot of running.

The story above is just one example of the kind of behavior that can become a serious problem—and a behavior that teachers and parents may not be able to identify at first. In the case of gravitational insecurity, the parent may be unaware of the issue because the child is pretty good at navigating around his home. The parent doesn't see the behavior that the teacher sees in the classroom. When the teacher experiences that behavior in class, he or she may never have heard of gravitational insecurity. What can happen in an instance like this? Well, everybody can wind up blaming the child. They begin to regard this child as a "bad kid." There's no question that we're talking about teachers and parents who love children. The issue here is this very troubling behavior: like a child screaming uncontrollably or running around a classroom with arms out so other children wind up getting touched or hit. It's puzzling. It's troubling. And there's a tendency to blame the child, even if we love the child.

One reason this can happen is that adults tend to take a child's social-emotional reactions personally. They assume the child is responding to them personally and, over time, they begin to feel as though this particular child is "out to get them." A teacher may not know very much about the child's parents but begin to assume that the problem is at home: he or she may start assuming that the child comes from a "bad family." These negative assumptions can begin to take shape, and they add to the overall stress. So it's a big step when Alejandra or Bronwyn arrive with a compassionate new perspective, saying things like, "I wonder if this child simply can't control this behavior. Let's get to the bottom of this misbehavior. Maybe this child is frightened." The understanding of the situation begins to shift right away. New questions are asked. The adults begin to move away from feelings of blame and shame. There's relief as the team begins to discuss helpful responses.

In another case, there was a child who would burst out screaming, twice a day, in the middle of class. It was uncontrollable when it happened, and oddly enough, it only happened twice each day. Eventually, the adults realized that their building was near a facility where heavy trucks came and went twice a day. It was the loud noise of these passing trucks, twice a day, that triggered the child's response. The other children and adults in the building had grown so accustomed to the noise that they didn't even notice it—but this boy was very aware of this sensation and was terrified by it. He wasn't a bad kid. He wasn't doing this in response to anyone in the classroom. Understanding the situation from a completely new perspective made a huge difference in that class. The trucks still roared past, but the teacher could now recognize that for a moment, twice a day, she need pay special attention to calming this boy's fear.

There are so many issues that can arise around sensory awareness and social-emotional development. Once we received a typical call that said, "We need help. This child is hitting other children and won't stop!" Well, it turned out that the boy in question had a particularly intense sensitivity to being touched by other people. As children move around a classroom, they often touch each other. It's normally not an issue, but in this particular child's development, he perceived even a casual brush or a simple touch as someone hitting him. That's how a touch felt to him. So he reacted by reaching out and hitting back. This was a developmental issue that eventually the child could learn to cope with, but at the moment Christine's team was called, it was a serious problem. Eventually, once the teacher understood what was going on, she could do things like ensure that this child was at the end of a line when the kids were lining up for an activity. That way, the child wasn't as likely to experience the kind of touching that he might if he were in the middle of the line of kids. The teacher also was able to use a deep touch to calm the child, which involved facing the child and pressing down firmly on his shoulders in a reassuring way. Deep-touch pressure might also take the form of a weighted blanket for rest time in the classroom, so a child can wrap up in the blanket to calm down his nervous system.

Parents may assume that trained teachers should be able to respond to whatever they experience in a class, but that's just not a realistic assumption. Teachers cannot hope to manage classrooms without some help from time to time, particularly when children are experiencing social-emotional challenges. In our area, when a teacher calls in Christine Zimmerman's team, that teacher is calling on experts in the field. A lot of teachers and parents experience her team as "the problem solvers." Her team steps in to support teachers with challenges that they can't resolve alone. The larger context here is that many educators today are overwhelmed by the number of children in their classes and by the range of special needs they are seeing in children. So, through Macomb Family Services, teachers in our area now have a chance to call in experts. Then, when someone from the team arrives, they don't simply dive in with an immediate response; they carefully observe and ask questions. Many times, they don't accept the first answer that comes to mind. They go back and carefully analyze what's happening. And they involve everyone in planning what will happen next. The teacher feels supported, winds up with a successful outcome in most cases, and the parents are relieved as well.

Sometimes the symptoms consultants observe in the classroom are intense. When we assess situations, we don't just look at symptoms—we look at the intensity and duration of symptoms. Do we see this troubling behavior 10 percent of the time? Or do we see this all day long? With the assessment tools this team uses, and then with the network of possible referrals they have at hand, sometimes the conclusion is that this is just a developmental stage that will pass with some helpful response from teachers and parents. But occasionally, we identify a child with greater challenges such as autism, where more referrals are needed.

Generally, teachers experience our help as a relief and many teachers have come to trust us. It takes a huge learning curve to understand the wide range of issues we encounter. But we believe that a socially and emotionally prepared child is a prepared learner. Or, another way to think of this is: **You can have the greatest educational programs in the world, but it's not going to do a bit of good if the child is not socially and emotionally able to sit in a classroom and participate.**

Most parents experience our help in the same way: as relief. We come to help and we often bring in other helpers as well.

From Alejandra Medina

Parents use the word "relief" to often describe our support, whether through our workshops, our classroom work or our home visits. Think about this for a moment, from the parents' perspective: If they have a child who starts screaming every time they step into a store, then the parents can't seem to win! If they let this tantrum continue, then people will point because they seem like "bad parents." On the other hand, if a mother tries to discipline her child in public, people may point and think she's bad for that reason. Whatever these parents do, they are criticized. This becomes a big emotional weight for the adults who really do love and care for their children.

I was working with a mother who had a 4-year-old child who was misbehaving—and this was particularly distressing for her because this was her sixth child. She was an experienced mother. The other five children didn't behave like this and she wasn't doing anything differently with the sixth one. Through observation and assessment the child was diagnosed with autism.

Occasionally, our work in classrooms and homes identifies children diagnosed with autism. Experts still don't know everything about autism, including exactly what causes it. Signs and symptoms of autism can vary greatly. Some children with autism are extremely aggressive, while others aren't so aggressive. Of course, we do recognize common signs such as issues with eye contact and socializing with other children. But it can be difficult, in a big class of young children, to pick up on what's happening.

It takes some expert help. Without a careful assessment, research studies have shown, a lot of children with autism would not be identified. Here's a common situation: A parent may laugh when a child does something funny. She thinks she's encouraging the child, but a child with autism may not read her laughter as supportive. That child might misinterpret the friendly social cue as someone laughing at him in an embarrassing way. The parent may not even be thinking about autism and, more likely, she ends up thinking that the child's negative reaction is misbehavior aimed at her, personally.

When this mother of the 4-year-old said she was happy to finally learn that her child was diagnosed with autism, she was describing the relief she was feeling at finally understanding his behavior after struggling with it for four years. Now, she understood the reason she was seeing this behavior—and she now knows about resources she can turn to for help with her child. Today, there are many options for help available for children with autism that weren't available years ago, including lots of things that parents can do at home to help their children respond to either under-stimulation or over-stimulation. We had helped this mother to put on a new set of glasses as she looked at this sixth child.

From Christine Zimmerman

Here's another way to think about this idea of "new glasses:"

Social psychologists have a term, "attribution theory," that is a research-based theory describing our natural tendency to attribute meaning to behavior. Then, based on what we think the behavior means, we respond in some way. An essential part of the work we do with parents and teachers is helping them to attribute a new and different meaning to the behavior they're experiencing with these children. Once the adult comes to a clearer understanding of the meaning behind the behavior, they're in a much better position to respond in a supportive and effective way.

Here's a very common example from our parenting workshops: A parent will complain that their 2-year-old is becoming a problem because, "Whatever I ask her to do, she says: 'No!'"

That parent is attributing the child's behavior to disrespect and defiance. If that's the case, than the parent may want to punish the child or to use some other method to teach the child more respect. But, in fact, negativism is a completely normal stage of early childhood development. It's just part of early childhood for these young children to discover that they have power and can say, "No!" If the parent understands that what is happening is just a phase, than they won't think of this behavior as a personal insult and they are likely to respond in a more helpful way, such as offering two acceptable choices.

The same thing is true when parents complain about young children putting their fingers in their mouths. Our experience tells us that children use their mouths to explore, self-soothe, increase sensory input, ease tooth discomfort or out of habit from earlier developmental stages. Their purpose is not necessarily to be gross, spread germs or act like a baby. There is likely an underlying need that needs to be addressed. There are many ways we can respond to help support children.

Teaching Self-Regulation: From Yoga to Tucker Turtle

Over the past two decades, a wealth of research has pointed toward the value of self-regulation in learning. Some adults have developed their own form of self-regulation, as a natural part of growth and maturity. According to the Illinois Early Learning Project,[1] the components of self regulation include the ability to "calm themselves, control their behavior and focus on tasks." A consensus among early childhood experts now tells us that we can make a big difference in the life of a struggling child by actively teaching them techniques that promote their own self-regulation. This is also in keeping with a Macomb Family Services' goal of finding and recommending to parents and teachers inexpensive ways that they can respond in order to help

_____

1 http://illinoisearlylearning.org/tipsheets/self.htm

children with their social-emotional development. This book isn't the place for a detailed exploration of this complex realm of learning; if you care to read more, you will find many recent books and journal articles on the subject. This is a practical book to share some of our best ideas with readers, so in the next few pages, we will describe two examples of activities that we've found are successful in encouraging self-regulation.

From Jennifer Whitcher, preschool director for a Great Start Readiness Program (GSRP) in Eastpointe, Michigan

There are so many ways to help children understand and regulate their emotions!

Alejandra is wonderful at showing us all sorts of simple techniques. I like to bring her in to work with the entire class each year because we learn something new from her every time. I remember one activity in which she simply crumbled paper as a way to deal with emotions—and I've seen her use squishy balls and stuffed animals, too—and that shows the class the many ways to use things around them to help calm their emotions.

We see a lot of children who come to us with emotional issues, and they haven't yet developed a way to express those feelings or to let them go. I remember, some years ago, I had one class with children who had anger issues—and I thought I was going to lose my mind! Then Alejandra came to my class, week after week, and that was such a source of relief. She showed the whole class techniques for anger management like standing up and pressing against a wall with all our might. Instead of letting go of anger by hitting another child, she challenged the kids to use all of their energy to see how hard they could push against the wall. This fit perfectly because at that age, they're fascinated with, How strong am I? Can I show off my muscles? The children were eager to try this technique. They loved it. And, after she left the classroom, we had this new way to release anger without hitting.

There is a multitude of methods and materials that Alejandra uses in the classroom: books, songs, activities. The techniques she shows the children really do help them to calm down so they feel better. I remember we once put on a puppet show in which two different puppets were hitting and shoving each other and stealing toys from each other. She got the children to talk about what else they could do to express themselves, rather than shoving or taking toys. Another time, we made face masks of monsters with different expressions to show whether they were glad or sad. The children responded to that, too, and we were able to have a very good talk about the masks as well as their own emotions. Later, we could return to that experience with the masks as a reminder.

From my perspective, Alejandra is spectacular. Of course, her goal is often giving the kids techniques they can use to regulate their own emotions and to relieve their stress. But I have to say: She relieved my stress, too! We became a happier class after she visited us.

Children exploring emotions with monster masks at a local preschool.

Yoga

From Debbie Giddey, a lead GSRP teacher in Warren, Michigan

As teachers, we try to understand the challenges we face in a classroom: we understand the stages of early childhood development, and we're always trying to use "best practices" with each child. Think about this situation: One child in the classroom is acting out by hitting other kids and sometimes even throwing things. Very quickly, you wind up spending your whole day focusing on this one child and his behavior. It feels like you're constantly putting out fires. Most veteran teachers can think of experiences like this. You're a professional and you love children, but you find yourself at home in the evening, thinking: "Oh, that boy is going to show up again at 7:30 tomorrow morning and he'll be with me until 5 p.m. Oh, another day of this! How am I going to get through it?" There are mornings when you can find yourself dreading your drive to work. Now, if I find myself in that situation, I know that I can call on the Macomb Family Services team and they will come in, they will help me understand what is happening and they will share some fresh ideas.

One of the most important things the MFS team does is teach children how to regulate their own feelings—including their anger. This process helps children become better socialized with their friends and the adults around them. I remember an eight-week series of visits by Bronwyn when I had one very challenging child in the class who needed individual help on anger management and socialization. Of course, Bronwyn is so good at what she does that all the children love it when they see her walk through the door. She usually brings a book with her, to go along with whatever we are working on that week: songs, movement or other activities.

One of the most effective techniques she brought to class was a book about yoga and a follow-up yoga activity for the class. That was very helpful for all of the children.

From Bronwyn Johnston

Imagine being a teacher in a classroom with 16 children who are unable to settle down at nap time. These 4-year-olds are getting off their cots to talk with friends, tossing and turning, climbing on classroom furniture and throwing their blankets. It's a common scenario and illustrates the problems that can arise when children lack self-regulation. In fact, in most of the classrooms we work in, self-regulation is a challenge. Teachers feel frustrated because they are trying to meet academic goals, while children are distracting each other by tossing things, rolling on the floor, crying or walking away during a story or instruction time. In response to this situation, we use many research-based tools and techniques to improve self-regulation skills within the classroom. Some of these tools and techniques include building emotional literacy, teaching direct regulation techniques (such as Tucker Turtle) and helping the children to practice mindfulness. Research at several universities—including the University of California, Berkeley—has demonstrated the benefit of teaching mindfulness practices for students' physical and psychological health, social skills and overall academic performance. Within our team, we have introduced a range of these techniques: mindful listening, guided imagery, progressive relaxation, self-affirmation mantras and yoga.

One aspect of mindfulness that many teachers find helpful is progressive relaxation. For example, the book *When the Anger Ogre Visits* by Andree and Ivette Salom helps children to understand anger and gives them tools to deal with it. One teacher found that by following the relaxation steps outlined in the book before rest time, most of the class fell asleep quickly. That has become a regular part of that teacher's daily routine with children.

We also use guided imagery. While visiting a classroom, we might play calming instrumental music and read a script designed to calm the children by promoting a feeling of safety and being loved. In one classroom, where the teacher had reported problems with nap time over a five-month period, this technique resulted in every single child falling asleep. What a relief for that teacher and those children!

Yoga is now popular with children, teachers and parents. Recent reports from the Pew Research Center mirror other nationwide studies that show a widespread, favorable interest in yoga among Americans of all ages. One of the biggest studies showing the growing use of yoga was summarized in a 2015 report from the National Institutes of Health, an agency of the United States Department of Health and Human Services. This summary was based on the department's National Health Interview Survey (NHIS), for which tens of thousands of Americans were interviewed:

> More Americans of all ages are rolling out their yoga mats in an effort to improve their health. ... Approximately 21 million adults (nearly double the number from 2002) and 1.7 million children practiced yoga. Children whose parents use a complementary health approach like yoga are more likely to use one as well. The increase in yoga has occurred across all age, racial, and ethnic groups. Most notably, the largest shift in the use of any mind and body approach was seen in the demographics of people using yoga:
>
> Among Americans age 18–44, yoga use nearly doubled since 2002;
>
> Among older Americans age 45–64, usage increased from 5.2 percent in 2002 to 7.2 percent in 2012; and
>
> Approximately 400,000 more children aged 4-17 used yoga in 2012 than in 2007.
>
> The high rates of use may be partly due to a growing body of research showing that some mind and body practices can help manage pain and reduce stress. Another factor that may have influenced the increased popularity of yoga is increased access—for instance, industry reports show that the number of yoga studios in the United States has increased substantially in recent years.

There certainly are lots of yoga resources all across the country! At Macomb Family Services, one of our favorite resources is the colorful, easy-to-understand guide called *Yoga Pretzels: 50 Fun Yoga Activities for Kids and Grownups*. Some yoga poses encourage children's focus and make them feel strong, while "Bear Breath" helps them to relax for rest time. Some classrooms have embraced the five steps in the *Calm Down Yoga for Kids* series, which pairs calming poses such as "Warrior 2" with self-affirmations. Many children enjoy moving their bodies in new ways and feeling "grown up" while doing it. Teachers regularly tell us that the yoga helps and that they are able to use some of those techniques to calm children before large group instruction and transitions.

The good news is: You can use our suggestions or find your own yoga resources! If you are inspired to add yoga to your classroom techniques, you'll find many options available for training, reading and classroom lessons.

*Two moms show off Tucker Turtles they made in one of
our Positive Solutions Parenting Workshops.*

Tucker Turtle

From Debbie Giddey

Kids remember Tucker Turtle for a long time! And he is so
simple to make. We take a paper plate and some cutouts of a
turtle head and legs. We use brass fasteners to attach the pieces
to the paper plate—so the children can rotate Tucker's legs and
feet so they seem to disappear under the shell like a real turtle.
Then we read Tucker's story and talk about responding to our
feelings like a turtle.

You can get very creative in making Tucker by decorating his
paper plate shell in various ways. When they're finished, kids just
love being able to move Tucker's legs and his head. Long after
that Tucker lesson, the story of Tucker remains in the classroom.
Weeks may pass and there will be some situation in which a

child reminds us about Tucker. Parents will tell me they've heard about Tucker at home.

The story is so simple. It starts this way:

> Tucker Turtle is a terrific turtle. He likes to play with his friends at Wet Lake School. But sometimes, things happen that can make Tucker really mad. When Tucker got mad, he used to hit, kick, or yell at his friends. His friends would get mad or upset when he hit, kicked, or yelled at them. Tucker now knows a new way to "think like a turtle" when something happens to make him mad. He can stop and keep his hands, body, and yelling to himself. … He can tuck inside his shell and take three deep breaths to calm down. …

From Jennifer Whitcher, preschool director for the Great Start Readiness Program

Oh, my! I just love Tucker! I love Tucker because he works so well and can make such a difference in a child's life. Tucker stays with kids because he's something they can see. A lot of preschoolers are visual learners. The whole experience with Tucker begins with a colorful story, which Alejandra uses to introduce Tucker to the class. Then the children make and decorate their own Tuckers with moveable legs and a head that can pivot around on the brass fasteners we use to attach them.

A while ago, I had a child come into a class with some serious emotional issues. Yelling was her first solution to every new problem. If something didn't go her way, she'd scream and sometimes she would hit. She had trouble even expressing what she wanted—or what problem she was facing. She just yelled. I remember that I was dealing with this situation sometime after Alejandra had already done the Tucker session that year. This little girl wasn't even present when the story was read; she hadn't made the craft. But we had some Tuckers in the classroom that other children had made. I remember I showed her another child's Tucker and I demonstrated how the legs and the head moved. I told the story to her. And this turned out to be the best thing in the world for her to discover! Tucker really calmed her down—more quickly than I'd ever seen her calm down before. She loved that the body parts could move and she demonstrated how she could do that herself—fold herself up like a turtle. Then she would breathe like Tucker and it would release her tension.

I then showed that little girl how to make her own Tucker. She not only made one—she carried that thing around with her wherever she went. She remembered that story and the experience for a long time. Much later, I could just say one word to her—"Tucker"—and she'd make the motions and do the breathing.

From Christine Zimmerman

We have found that the use of Tucker Turtle has been a very effective tool in promoting positive ways for children to learn manage their strong feelings. Another benefit to teachers and parents in using Tucker is that it is available at no cost to them. He's funded through a five year grant to the Center on the Social Emotional Foundations for Early Learning through the Office of Head Start and the Child Care Bureau, and all the resources that teachers need to start using Tucker in a classroom are at Vanderbilt University's Center on the Social and Emotional Foundations for Early Learning website. You can find a PowerPoint presentation of the Tucker story both in English and Spanish, plus ideas for teaching about Tucker and a printable PDF pattern of the body parts, at http://csefel.vanderbilt.edu/resources/strategies.html.

Look around that web page and you will find lots of other materials as well. Check out the links in the left margin of that web page—such as the "For Teachers/Caregivers" link. You will find some good suggestions for books and activities on social-emotional development. Also available on the website are stories about being a friend, using words, and other feelings and experiences. Some of these resources are intended for use individually—with children who have challenging behaviors and need help understanding their feelings and finding different ways to respond. There are also feelings charts and problem-solving tools. Most of the materials are available in both English and Spanish.

Play and Learn: Parents and Children Learning Together

Today, everyone seems to be promoting the value of Play and Learn. In Washington, D.C., the United States Department of Health and Human Services (HHS) recommends this kind of program to enhance parents' interactions with their infants, toddlers and preschoolers. Play and Learn programs can strengthen the attachment between parent and child and can stimulate early language and cognitive and social development, HHS says. Internationally, the United Nations has recognized play as so important to human development that they say an opportunity to play should be regarded as a universal right for children.

From Christine Zimmerman

The Play and Learn groups through our Macomb Family Services Early Learning Communities provide valuable support, education and resources on early childhood development, appropriate expectations of children and age-appropriate activities. These groups are valuable for increasing positive interactions between parents and caregivers and their children—and for promoting children's social-emotional development. Our Play and Learn groups are designed so that each person who attends will leave having learned something new. The hands-on activities we provide in class are easily duplicated at home. The weekly group is a place where caregivers and parents gain confidence in teaching their children skills that they might not explore at home, such as cutting with scissors for fine motor development. Through the support of the facilitator, families overcome fears. Many gain a wide range of insights, including how to introduce and practice new skills; the importance of schedules and routines; and better techniques for disciplining children. They also build strong relationships with other families. In our Play and Learn groups, developmental screenings are completed to increase the parents' knowledge of appropriate expectations for their children and to address any potential developmental delays as early as possible.

From Theresa Swalec, principal of Westview Elementary School and Early Childhood Center in Warren, Michigan

When children finally start preschool, we can see the difference in children who have had earlier experiences with Play and Learn groups: they're more aware; there's an easier separation from the parent; they're used to a routine and to classroom settings. Play and Learn is hugely beneficial. Perhaps the biggest benefit is that parents become more aware of how important it is for them to be directly involved in their child's education. They're actively participating in Play and Learn; they're able to compare experiences with other parents and children; and there's no distraction from TV, phones or other technology while they are in the group.

If you're an experienced parent, you may not realize how difficult it is for first-time parents to learn about all of the possible activities that they can do with their children. When La Don Williams passes out a simple recipe for Play-Doh—out of things most people already have in their kitchens—that's a huge discovery for many families! Some parents seem to know all the popular songs that we use to get children actively involved in the group, but a lot of parents have never heard those songs. So, another big contribution comes through all of the new ideas and the music we send home with the families who participate. Kids certainly remember the songs we sing during Play and Learn sessions, even if their parents forget them! Parents tell us all the time that their children just won't stop singing them. Or think for a moment about something as basic as reading a book with a child. As a parent, you may know how to do this basic activity very effectively, but a lot of parents never had someone read to them on a regular basis. So, at every Play and Learn, La Don is modeling good ways to read books with children. Watching her, the parents are learning as much as their children are about the process of reading. Sometimes La Don shows parents activities that they'd never imagined—like playing with shaving cream. That's so popular! Shaving cream can be sprayed onto a washable table and children invited to play with it by spreading it around, making pictures in it or writing their names in it.

So many senses are involved with shaving cream: the touch and feel of the cream, the skills that can be used in moving it around and even the smell of the stuff. Parents will tell us, "That was so much fun in this class, but I'm not doing that on my table at home." And we say, "Instead, why don't you try it in the bathtub at bath time?" That's very easy. Parents take all of these ideas and examples home with them. In our groups, we also see a lot of single parents who don't have much parenting support when they get home. When they come to our center for a Play and Learn, they get to know other parents who are learning the same things. We often see them setting up their own play dates with other parents and children in the group. We know they're continuing to share the techniques they're learning.

These groups also are a great way for us to help parents identify developmental delays or other issues. Sometimes, in a Play and Learn group, issues are identified that the parents hadn't even considered. I know that if La Don identifies a significant developmental delay, for example, she will talk to the parent and provide referrals for more evaluation and help for the family. If we recognize these issues early in a child's life, we can help the family in many ways. I've seen children with significant delays at 3 or 4 years of age who receive referrals through Play and Learn—and then get the extra help they need. The result can be that the child is able to have a normal, successful experience as they start school.

One reason why La Don is so successful is that she works with parents. She certainly knows all about early childhood, but she doesn't direct the parents—she works with them in a very engaging way. I've seen this kind of interaction many times. She always encourages parents to take the lead. She's patient. She's also just a fun person to be around and that good humor goes a long way toward making parents feel comfortable with her.

The screening tool to identify children at risk that Theresa Swalec is referring to is the standardized Ages and Stages Questionnaires®: Social Emotional (ASQ:SE), a widely used screening process in which a parent or a child's main caregiver responds to questions about behaviors they are observing. The basic ASQ was developed at the University of Oregon, based on research begun in the 1970s by Dr. Diane Bricker and further expanded in partnership with Dr. Jane Squires—both leading experts in this field. The first edition, called Ages & Stages Questionnaires (ASQ): A Parent-Completed Child-Monitoring System, debuted in 1995. The "SE" edition—a specialized form of the questionnaire designed to monitor social and emotional issues—was first released in 2002. Forms of the ASQ now are widely used in pinpointing developmental progress and catching potential delays in young children—thereby paving the way for meaningful next steps in learning, intervention or monitoring. Since the ASQ was developed, studies have shown that without such tools, less than half of developmental disabilities or mental health problems are identified in early childhood. With screening, the vast majority of such issues can be identified at an early stage. A version of the basic ASQ is available from United Way for Southeastern Michigan, at www.BibToBackpack.org.

From Gina Vatalaro, who has been such a regular participant in Play and Learn with her daughter, Cc, that Gina now also works as a child care provider during Macomb Family Services classes for parents

Cc and I have been going to La Don's Play and Learn for about two years, and I've seen Cc really blossom. She's now at the top of her class in preschool and I attribute that to all of the experiences we've had together in Play and Learn. She's become very outgoing. She'll walk up to welcome someone who's new in the group and say, "Hi, I'm Cc. That's with two 'C's." She's proud of that. When she was born, we thought about naming her Cecilia, but then we thought we'd probably start calling her CeeCee, so we thought we'd make it even simpler by spelling her name with just two 'C's. Of course, in English, people have trouble with a name that doesn't have any vowels. But in the end, it's become her trademark: "Hi, I'm Cc. That's with two 'C's."

You can probably tell that Cc and I like to be around other people. As a stay-at-home mom, I found myself craving adult interaction. When I found a chance to get out of the house for a regular playgroup, that was wonderful! At first, Cc and I went to another group that we liked. But then that group ended—and we discovered La Don's group, which we liked even better! For example: In our first group, after the circle time we would have maybe two centers with crafts and activities for the children. La Don usually has six centers set up each time! There are a lot more choices with this Play and Learn group.

As a parent, I'd say that one of the biggest advantages of Play and Learn is the many resources that I never had at home. Some of them we now bring home with us; some of them we just do at Play and Learn. Another advantage is that La Don is there to help coach us. For instance, Cc experienced a big challenge when learning to use scissors. Cc hadn't used scissors until about age 3, because scissors require a lot of hand and wrist coordination. I still remember when she first tried scissors at Play and Learn. She got so frustrated! She couldn't keep her wrist in the proper position and that meant she couldn't cut in a straight line. She tore the paper. She threw it down. She didn't want any help from me. She was just *done* with that activity! Well, I remember La Don talking to me about how difficult it is for a child to learn to use scissors. I don't think I had much patience with Cc about this until La Don told me that patience is exactly what I needed to develop in order to help her. She'd say, "Cool off. Take a breath. Do other things, then come back to this activity and try it again later." With patience and practice, I could get Cc to try it again. It wasn't easy. Learning to use scissors has been a long process, mainly because Cc doesn't enjoy doing things that frustrate her. However, I can see that the whole issue could have been a much bigger problem between Cc and me if La Don hadn't been there to talk me through the process.

Since that time, I've seen other moms and children trying to use scissors. Some of them hit the same point of frustration. I can remember one mom who said, "We're going to sit here and you're not going to move until you learn to use those scissors!" Her child was obviously frustrated. The mom was angry. But I was able to talk to this mom—personally speaking—about how hard it is for some children to learn to use scissors. I told her about Cc. I was able to help her calm down and have more patience.

Play and Learn may seem like a simple thing—some songs and stories and crafts. But it really is an opportunity for parents to open doorways into new worlds they might never have discovered without such opportunities. Play and Learn is great for helping our children learn to socialize, but it's also great for parental interaction as well. So many times, I've talked with other parents who are facing similar experiences. The conversations start like this: "I'm having a terrible time right now with potty training. How about you?" Or, "My two toddlers fight at home. Do your kids fight?" Or, "How do you get her to sleep at night? We're having bedtime problems." Or, "Do you try to regulate the television at home? How do you do it?" Or, "He won't give up that pacifier. Did you have a problem with that?"

As parents, we're all in the same boat. We all get lost sometimes. We all need someone to hold our hand, reassure us and give us some guidance. I like to help other parents and children if I can. La Don encourages me to do that. In fact, now I work with the Macomb Family Services team as a child care provider to take care of children during the parent workshops La Don teaches. After my experiences with La Don, I've realized that I'd like to go back to college, complete more classes and eventually get certified to run these kinds of groups.

What is Play and Learn, Exactly?

From Christine Zimmerman

What is Play and Learn? That's a challenging question—and somewhat difficult to answer. Look around and you will find countless groups that offer a huge range of activities for parents and children under this same "Play and Learn" title.

In the 1960s, educators rarely talked about "play and learn." The phrase was popularized in the 1970s and became a major trend from the late '70s through the '90s. Around 2000, the phrase surged again and, today, it is well known from coast to

Gina Vatalaro and her daughter Cc work with modeling clay at a Macomb Family Services Play and Learn session.

coast. That also means that some Play and Learn programs have been operating for more than three decades with resources that have changed dramatically during those years. If you experienced Play and Learn with your child in the '80s, the program may look much different if you are looking at it for a grandchild now.

If you search online, you'll find a huge variety of products labeled "Play and Learn." No one controls the trademark; there is no universally accepted list of best practices. There are Play and Learn books, music and accessories for young children like tote bags and even plastic activity trays to attach to car seats. There are educational Play and Learn toys like toy shopping baskets, colored chalk, blocks and musical instruments. The internet offers more than 6,000 products using some version of that label.

At Macomb Family Services, we offer Play and Learn with a wide range of activities to engage all of a young child's senses and their developing mind, muscles and coordination and social emotional skills. Engaging positive relationships between parents and children is a primary foundation to the Play and Learn group. We model and support parent skills of problem solving, communication, setting limits, and other essential life skills. The quality of interactions between parents and children are key to supporting their development. In planning each aspect of our activities, we draw on research-based principles. We have asked La Don Williams to share a description of how we organize our groups. Feel free to use this as a model, described below—or to compare this with other models in your part of the country. You can use our ideas, or adapt them to your own settings.

How We Organize Play and Learn

From La Don Williams

What do we mean by "play"?

The phrase "Play and Learn" sounds like a program only about children, but it's also designed to assist parents by modeling ways they can interact in hands-on ways with their children. Our sessions are uninterrupted time that parents and caregivers get to spend with their children. There's more depth to what is happening than parents may recognize at the beginning. A first-time parent may come with a child who loves to paint and, on that first visit, that's all the child wants to do. The parent may think: This is just a place to come and let my child have fun with painting,—something she may be hesitant to do at home because it's so messy. But, over time, we make it clear to our parents that each activity has a purpose. In playing with paint, I may have long pieces of paper set out and encourage the children to paint with long strokes. They're actually developing larger muscles as they paint that way. We encourage parents and children to try all the different activities we offer, because each one models a different kind of developmental skill.

We want our activities to be fun and playful as they teach important skills. Some of our structured activities promote small and large motor development, language development, cognitive development and social-emotional development. Activities can include numbers, letters and color recognition; music and movement; and even elementary science activities. We hope that families will then repeat some of what they experienced in class when they get home.

To put it simply: We want the parents to play, too. It's not just the children who learn from playing; parents learn, too. Let's take the example of painting. I encourage a parent not to stand over a child and tell him what to paint. Children don't have fun if adults are always directing exactly what they're supposed to be doing. It should be a joy to paint and the discoveries children make come automatically through the process of picking up a brush, dipping it in some paint and beginning to move that brush around. In fact, if a parent is overly directive with a child, I'll say something like, "Mom, paint your own picture. Go on. Pick up a brush and paint alongside your child." However, we don't want the parents to stand too far away; we want them at an eye-to-eye level with their children. If both parent and child are working at the same level, than they're more likely to have a conversation about what they're each painting. Playing together and having rich conversations are key to supporting positive interactions and relationships between parents and children.

How do we find an ideal place?

Starting a parent-and-child group is easier if you find the right location. You want a room that's kid-friendly and, specifically, preschool-friendly. The place should be welcoming for children with furniture that's their size. Ideal is a classroom or play space that already has things children like to play with, like colorful blocks.

Is the place safe? It's very important that parents feel safe bringing their young children. Dads sometimes participate, too, but the majority of our parent participants are moms who come alone with their children. Check out the ease and safety of the parking facilities. Inside your classroom, remember that parents are likely to want to set their coats and belongings to one side of the room as they sit down on the floor with their children for the activities. Is there a secure place for purses? Or can they put them in a spot where they can keep an eye on them during class?

Think about these questions, too: Is there enough space for all of the activities you want to offer? Is there a cozy area where parents and children can look at books? Will you have equipment like dry-erase boards and sturdy tables for wet and messy activities? Is there a comfortable carpeted area for circle time? Then, of course, you'll want to check out the restrooms: Are they easily accessible, safe and clean? Do the restrooms have changing tables and step stools?

How do we set up a schedule?

A consistent schedule helps parents make a habit of attending every session. Sometimes you'll have to change the schedule due to holidays or the availability of the building that is hosting your group, but try to keep changes to a minimum. A regular time and day, every week, maximizes a parent's ability to plan ahead.

We run our groups for 90 minutes once a week. Talk with parents you hope will attend your group about the best time of day. Parents with older children may have their daily schedules governed by the school times of older children. Parents also will prefer that Play and Learn not conflict with nap times. Find an ideal day and time—and stick to it as best you can.

Here is a sample of a flyer we distributed when we were scheduling a new Play and Learn group. Parents responded very well to this type of invitation:

We're very happy to have you and your little explorers join our program! Play and Learn groups are held once a week and last about 90 minutes. These are popular groups, so we encourage you to sign up for this new group right now to ensure we have enough space for everyone. A small snack is provided at most groups. If your child has any food allergies it is best that you bring your own snack. Each week has a different theme that will touch on subjects like beginning skills in math, reading, social-emotional development, art, gross motor and fine motor skills. Our activities are developmentally appropriate to help prepare your child for kindergarten. If you have any other questions please feel free to call or email Ms. La Don.

What do we play?

We use activities and lessons that research has shown will help in the various domains of early childhood learning, including physical development and health, social and emotional development, language development, creative expression and knowledge in literacy, math and science. We prefer activities that adults can repeat later, and we often provide handouts to encourage their use at home. Of course, the activities should be fun. Among our most popular activities are:

- Singing songs
- Doing finger plays
- Playing with scarves and other materials that provide opportunity for practicing rhythmic movement

- Using stickers and stamps
- Reading picture books—both fiction and nonfiction, and especially books about animals and about how things are made
- Painting with brushes, sponges and sometimes with nontraditional items
- Drawing with chalk, crayons or washable markers
- Playing games that encourage cooperation, patience and concentration
- Making crafts with natural, recycled and donated items, such as leaves, bottle tops, egg cartons, plastic water bottles, buttons, old keys, dried flowers, acorns and ribbon
- Doing puzzles, including floor puzzles with big pieces and age-appropriate puzzles with magnets or knobs on the pieces

How do we play?

During Play and Learn, the facilitator gently reminds adults to stay in what we describe as "a hug's reach of your child." Although social interaction is encouraged in our groups, it's easy for adults to get caught up in their own conversations and lose track of what the children are doing. So the facilitator reminds adults that they have activities to complete alongside their children, and this helps them stay focused on our Play and Learn style of play.

The facilitator of the Play and Learn group not only prepares lessons that are age-appropriate for the children in the group, but also educates the parents and caregivers on the early child-hood development that is taking place. The facilitator coaches parents on having meaningful conversations with their children, providing tips such as getting down on the child's level, repeating what the child says and asking for more information. We encourage parents to start their interactions with open-ended questions and observations, such as:

- Can you tell me more about … ?
- How did you … ?
- Can you show me … ?

- It looks like you …
- What was your favorite part of … ?
- What do you think will happen if … ?
- Where did you get the idea to … ?

How do we start our sessions?

We begin our sessions by welcoming people as they arrive, forming a circle, singing songs, sharing stories and going over our plans for our time together. First, parents sign in as they arrive; while the group is forming, we ask parents to look at the books we have provided for the children. If we have a particular theme for the session—frogs, for example—than we try to bring out books that feature frogs. Once everyone has arrived, we move into our circle on the floor. Don't wait too long for this to happen, or parents will think that you have moved your start time and they will begin arriving later and later.

Sometimes, new children who have never attended a circle time will find it difficult to join the rest of our group. If that happens, ask the new parents to sit where their child feels comfortable—perhaps outside the circle—and have them try to do the activities along with the rest of the group. It may take a couple of visits to the group, but these parents and children almost always manage to join the circle after the children feel comfortable with the weekly routine.

Learning the names of the children is very important. We start with a greeting song and make a point of welcoming each child by name. If you are a facilitator with a poor memory for names, ask the parents to help you by making nametags for their children. Children love to hear favorite songs repeated week after week. That way they know what to expect and can enthusiastically participate. This also is the time when we might offer a finger play, encouraging parents and children to do the finger play along with the leader. By repeating these activities, parents also are developing their own repertoire to use at home. If you add a new song, consider repeating it three times: once to introduce the song; the second time to let the children practice; and the third time to have everyone fully join in the singing. Help parents connect what they are learning with daily opportunities to interact further with their children. Make suggestions to the parents about places where they can use these songs and simple rhythmic activities with their children—while waiting in line somewhere, while sitting in the doctor's office and so on. You might even get the children involved in choosing songs by encouraging them to make a songbook. Or write the names of songs on sticks and let children choose the next song to sing from among the colorful song sticks.

During circle time, we include lots of movement. Depending on the age and interest of the children, we may use colored scarves, pom-poms or other inexpensive objects that make rhythmic movement more fun.

While still in the circle, we also explain the activities that the families will be able to explore during the rest of the day's session. If they have an opportunity to create a craft related to the day's theme, we show an example of that craft and explain how it can be assembled. We always encourage each parent to follow the child's lead, which usually means that the children won't complete all of the available activities that day. Reassure parents that this is fine. It's not like school, in which all students are expected to complete all assignments. This is a time for exploration because the best learning happens when children are free to follow their own interests.

What are our activities?

Some Play and Learn programs offer one or two activities for children. We believe that it's important to have many activities, so children of all developmental levels and interests will find something fun to explore. We also aren't afraid of messy activities—in fact, we encourage parents to cheer along with their children's experimentation, even if little hands get covered in paint or shaving cream or paste. One solution is to have lots of baby wipes available!

We already have described many of the general options we offer our children each week, so here are some specific examples of how we adapted our activities to a special one-week theme about frogs:

For tactile and math development, we put many colors of plastic frogs in a pile of artificial green grass on top of a wide, round table. We used the inexpensive plastic grass sold for Easter baskets. Then, we put big cups and tweezers on the table. Children were challenged to find the frogs in the grass. We urged parents to ask about the frogs' colors. Children sorted the frogs by size and color. They put them in cups and counted them. They dumped the cups and filled them again.

At our painting center, we provided yellow and blue paint and big sheets of paper. Parents helped children explore the paints, which, of course, can turn into a bright frog-green if mixed. Children played with the colors and discovered various shades of green that they could paint onto their papers.

We set up a collage center with many green materials: green ribbons, paint samples, colored paper and sequins. Adults helped the children get started by squeezing the glue and sticking materials to the collage paper. We also encouraged parents to focus on green things: go on a "green hunt" and find things around the house that are green; wear green colors; and eat green foods.

For math, we laid out lily pads with big numbers on them, along with more plastic frogs. Parents prompted children to help the appropriate number of frogs hop onto each matching numbered lily pad. We encouraged parents to take the lily pad and jumping ideas home with them. Jump like frogs. Count your jumps. Make your own lily pad.

Letter recognition was focused on "Ff is for frog." In one center we had paper and lots of materials— such as pictures of frogs—that children could cut out with scissors and paste onto a paper labeled with the letter "F."

The center also had frog-shaped cookie cutters. We offered small, plastic frogs that parents could hide in Play-Doh for the children to find. Then, we encouraged kids to hide the frogs.

After reading this list, are you developing your own ideas? We are constantly changing our list of activities and adding things based on weekly themes, seasons of the year and the availability of simple, inexpensive materials that are ideal for children. We have made creative use of blocks, puzzles, white boards, markers, soap and water in a big tub—and lots of pretend play items that can expand a child's imagination even further.

When planning your own activities, remember that a regular schedule of transition times is important to both children and their parents. When this schedule is established, everyone gets to know when circle time begins and ends, week after week; when the activities will end; when we will pass out a snack and when we'll start wrapping up the session. The facilitator should pay close attention to marking these transitions for the families. To keep everyone aware of the schedule, we typically say something like, "Five minutes until we start cleaning up!"

How do we close out a session?

We regularly sing cleanup songs, over and over, which gives parents direction on how to help their children clean up the play area. If you've got paper scattered across the floor, make picking up the paper a part of the song. Parents often tell us that they find themselves repeating our cleanup songs at home.

Before our snack and final story, we do expect parents and children to help clean up any toys or materials that have been used during our activities. We also help the children wash their hands before the snack. We don't regard the snack as an essential part of a successful session, but we do usually provide one. If you have the resources, snack time is a great opportunity to encourage children to try healthy foods they might not have tasted at home.

Reading a picture book during this closing time is an opportunity to model for parents how to interactively read with young children—and we've found that parents simply enjoy listening, too. Choose a special song to be sung at the end of each class. As they're ready to leave, give each child a sticker or stamp. If you have access to age-appropriate books, give each child a book to take home to add to their family library. In time, the children come to expect the book and often are so excited that they insist their parents read the book before they even leave the site.

#LIVEINTHED
BIB TO BACKPACK PROGRAM
UNITED WAY

Care to watch a TV news clip that features several minutes with La Don and one of her Play and Learn groups? Check out http://www.clickondetroit.com/news/live-in-the-d-bib-to-backpack-program.

"Give Parents Credit"

From Owen Pfaendtner, CEO of Macomb Family Services

The title of this book really captures what we do: We are building healthy relationships in early learning. We're doing that by focusing on the social-emotional health and the school readiness of young children. That pretty much sums up our story. The theme of relationships, in particular, really resonates with me as a cornerstone of our work over many years. These days, with reduced funding for many programs across the country, it's more important than ever for people to come out of their silos and help each other. We need to form working partnerships, share ideas like we are doing in the pages of this book—and work together to ensure that families can find the help they need wherever they live.

Nationwide, the complexities of family life are surfacing new kinds of problems. Decades ago, not many families enrolled their children in preschool; now, preschool is a common part of childhood and preschool teachers are spotting problems that, years ago, no one may have noticed until children tried to start school. At the same time, research is demonstrating the value of new kinds of programs to help with those new challenges we are identifying. As Christine and La Don pointed out earlier in this chapter, no one was even talking about "play and learn" in the 1960s. Today, if it's done well, a Play and Learn program facilitates screenings and activities that research shows us will help identify and address developmental delays early.

Ultimately, you've got to give parents credit. Overall, parents are a lot more educated now about raising kids than they ever were before. Everywhere you turn, the importance of reading to children is stressed by educators, community leaders and celebrities. I don't remember that much emphasis on parents reading to their children when I was growing up, in the '60s. Today, though, most parents know they should be reading at home. Parents already know a lot and that's why we work together with them, drawing on their strengths.

But we all have to remember one thing: No one is born knowing how to be a parent. Somebody has to teach and mentor new parents. As community leaders, we've got to give them opportunities to find out what will help them to become better parents. Early education for parents is a huge advantage for every kid in America.

Our Resources

"Planting Healing Seeds"

From Dr. Robert J. Wicks, a clinical psychologist, teacher and author of more than a dozen books on resilience and well-being, including The Resilient Clinician, Bounce: Living the Resilient Life *and* Perspective: The Calm Within the Storm *.* **Based in Pennsylvania, Wicks travels widely as a speaker and workshop leader for caregivers, and his audiences often consist of men and women in the armed forces, in social work, in education, public safety, medical professions and in governmental service.**

This book comes out of Michigan at the right time. Wherever I travel around the world, I find people who are doing very difficult work to help people in need—but they often find that their biggest challenge is finding the resiliency to keep going with their work, day after day. I am a caregiver for other caregivers. I work with highly motivated individuals who often are serving in communities where so much trauma surrounds them that they wind up feeling fatigued. Sometimes, they are so drained that they feel like failures, even when it's obvious to me that they are not.

First, what these individuals need is a new perspective. This group in Michigan—Macomb Family Services—talks about the need to help people "put on a new set of glasses." I call that *perspective*. And, I can tell you: It's such a powerful idea that I've written an entire book on the psychological value of gaining a new perspective. In the opening lines, I tell readers, "When someone gains or regains a healthy sense of perspective, it feels like pure magic. The person sees more clearly and experiences greater freedom. Unforeseen possibility surfaces. New peace and joy are seeded."

What this organization in Michigan understands is that zeroing in on its overall mission in the community starts with building strong relationships within the team. Christine started this process at Macomb Family Services by inviting the early childhood team to take time to discern how their individual sense of mission fits into the group's overall mission. They also take time to stop, to reflect and to periodically revisit their mission. Then, their team members work with their clients to frame their purpose. And the frame they are setting does not sound like the typical frame for success these days: wealth, prestige, fame, and influence. They're doing something that is very countercultural.

In this process, they're not asking, "How much do you hope to earn?" "What do you hope to own?" "How far do you hope to climb over others?" Instead, they're asking, "What are my Signature Strengths?" "What is my personal mission?" There are other terms that could also be used for this process of discernment. I would put the question this way: "What are my charisms?" Then, once the individuals in the team have a renewed sense of their strengths—alternatively, I might call this a sense of their mission, or of their charisms—then they connect their charisms to help all of the people who come to their agency in the best ways possible.

That formulated approach is different than the standard formula for success often implemented these days. This is one reason that caregivers who are fatigued or who have gone through trauma in their work often start to think that they have failed. They don't understand that as caregivers, we are not in the "success" business. We are in the *faithfulness* business.

One of the most important steps in this countercultural process is intentionally giving people the time to stop and seriously reflect. In this group in Michigan, the staff is regularly setting aside time for reflection. I've written and talked a lot about the need to find time for reflection, because I've found that people around the world identify this as one of their greatest challenges.

When I was invited to speak to members of the U.S. Congress and their chiefs of staff, I asked them: "What's the greatest problem you face today?" They could have said anything—war, poverty, the economy—anything. Instead, someone said, "The biggest problem is that there's not enough time to stop and read everything that crosses our desks. And there's not enough time to stop and think." What he was saying was: There's not enough time to reflect. And that's not just a problem for members of Congress. That's true for so many caregivers around the world. Intentionally making time for people to stop and reflect is another countercultural value.

There are dark alleys that can lead us astray while in reflection. I've written and taught a lot about this. We can get lost in what I call the "silver casket of nostalgia;" or, simply put, we can spend too much time lost in fantasies about the future—fantasies that focus on all the wonderfully unrealistic things that might happen someday. In addition to the silver casket, two of the darkest alleys are arrogance—which really is an unhealthy projection of blame on others—and discouragement, which comes from a need for immediate gratification and an unrealistic desire for definitions of success that are unattainable. We have to encourage people to use their time for reflection in positive ways. What Christine is encouraging is what I call a *spirit of intrigue*. We need to fill ourselves with a fresh spirit of intrigue, asking questions such as: "Who am I?" "What are my talents?" "Where are my growing edges?" When you are intrigued about yourself, your organization and the clients you serve, then you can renew your spirit to the point that you step out into the world again, asking: "What can I do to help?"

Christine is offering an opportunity for people to become intrigued about how their own mission can connect with the missions of others around them. It's an opportunity for real friendship, collaboration and community. That process dramatically changes one's perspective. You begin to realize that when your limited efforts come together with other people's limited efforts in the right way, remarkable things can be accomplished. That process leads to real passion.

During the Vietnam War, the children of Vietnam grew up with so many traumas that it seemed impossible to help them. Eventually, Thich Nhat Hạnh took some of the survivors of the war to Plum Village, a Buddhist meditation center he co-founded in France; but he did not deal directly with the trauma. Instead, his approach was to have the survivors become part of a community of reflection. When I visited with him, I asked about this approach. What was he doing? He answered, "We are planting healing seeds alongside their trauma. As they grow, the healing seeds will grow with them."

In offering friendship and community and an opportunity to become intrigued again about the possibilities of life, that's what we can do to help the world: Together, we can plant healing seeds.

Why Should I Create a Personal Mission Statement?

From Kathleen Macdonald, head of The Macdonald Group, a consulting firm in Ann Arbor, Michigan. She is an executive coach and consultant who works with clients around the world to manage internal transitions and external challenges that often result from changes in global culture.

Personal relationships are the foundation of every positive movement forward in one's life.

The early childhood group at Macomb Family Services has found the unique power in spending time thinking about and working on relationships. Within the early childhood team, this process begins when team members are asked to stop and figure out a personal mission statement. This organization has its own twist on this process: it is different than other so-called mission statements that groups—organizations or companies—often try to develop. Usually, the three questions asked when creating a group mission statement are:

- What do we do?
- How do we do it?
- Why do we do it?

They're asking people to periodically stop and think about questions like: "What on earth am I doing?" "How am I going to try to keep doing this work?" And, overall: "So, what am I all about?" "What's my best self?" "What are my strengths?" "How do I see myself as an individual within this organization?" And that all points to the question: "What's my preferred future?"

Encouraging reflection is important in an organization that works with clients, like Macomb Family Services does. This team of professionals goes out every day to help its clients see the world in a different way—so they, also, need to check in now and then; to reconfigure their own view of the world, and their place in that world. You can't help others reflect if you're not taking time for reflection yourself.

Macomb Family Services talks about "putting on new glasses." Most of us are familiar with a device called a phoropter, even if we don't recognize the name. It's the gadget that flips different lenses in front of our eyes at the ophthalmologist's office. A set of lenses are clicked into place and the doctor asks, "Which is better—A or B?" Then, the lenses are flipped again, and we're asked, "Which is better now—this one or that one?" You keep going through a series of lenses until, eventually, an image begins to form—and, before too long, you're seeing clearly. That's also true in working with members of a professional team. We need to make time to look at ourselves and at the work we're doing through a series of different lenses. We can look through the lens of age and emotional development, or through the lens of gender, power, status or income—you get the idea. We keep flipping the lenses until we're not guessing anymore about the work we're doing—or about the world around us in which we work. Through this process, we are coming closer and closer to clarity about our own lives, about the members of our team and about the world around us, where ultimately we're trying to help people.

These are just some of the insights that I'm seeing from this group. And it all starts with reflecting on what they call a personal mission statement—getting some clarity about themselves as individuals. It's a good process.

In a similar manner, I have reflective reminders that I keep in front of me daily—including in the front of my daily journal, where I write down everything I'm supposed to be doing each day. Mine says: "I share freely all that I know. I do it in a way that helps people gain their own insights. I do it with love and compassion mixed with honesty. I show love and care in all that I do and I try to enrich as many lives as I can."

The point is to keep it handy. In the Macomb offices, they hang these motivational reminders on the wall near their desks. I keep a second copy of my own reminders in my phone, so that I can look at it right there on the screen and ask myself: "Hey, how did I do today?" "Does this still express what I think I'm all about?" "How close did I come?"

Every once in a while, it's important to stop and do something like this. Ask yourself: "What's my preferred vision of my future?" Then, think about it: "OK, if that's my preferred vision of the future, then what am I going to do today to make that happen?"

Honestly, I'm not a huge fan of having big organizations write mission statements. I've helped lots of groups write them over the years, but there is a danger in the process. Big group mission statements can all too often wind up on these lovely plaques that everybody ignores soon after they're officially hung on the wall. What's intriguing about the process this Macomb group follows is that they own, individually, what they come up with in the process. They do it individually and then they hang these statements on the wall, letting everyone see what they believe that they can do and how they plan to do it. They're saying, to everyone else: "Hold me accountable to this."

That's why I think that personal mission statements may wind up being more valuable than organizational ones.

Creating Personal Mission Statements

From Christine Zimmerman, a licensed master social worker, is director of early childhood programming at Macomb Family Services.

At the core of the work we do is our strength-based perspective in relating to parents, teachers and children. For example, we use a strength-based assessment tool when we are invited into a home or a classroom to spend time with a child. We ask: "What strengths does this child have?" "How can we use those strengths to support change?" When we work with the members of our team at Macomb Family Services, we take the same approach.

Originally, I decided to engage in the process of creating personal mission statements because our team was experiencing many programmatic changes. Some of this turbulence was caused by our funders; some of it was our own internal questioning of our identity and efficacy. Since that time, preliminary evaluations of our work through the Social Innovation Fund (SIF) have shown that we are, indeed, very effective in the work that we do. But, at the time we created our mission statements, we were wrestling with rapidly evolving expectations and our own questions about our work. I decided that we needed to establish a clear piece of ground where our team could stand together, united with a renewed sense of competence, passion and vision for our collective next steps.

I organized a staff retreat, and part of that day was devoted to the process of writing personal mission statements. Our focus in creating these statements was greater clarity on what each of us meant when we talked about our individual talents; our purpose; and our assumptions about quality work on a daily basis. Even more importantly, these statements became expressions of passion. Without passion, we tend to fall back on "going through the motions." In that mode, professionals may still be effective— but our team expects a better outcome than that. We don't want to simply meet minimum expectations; we want to exceed them

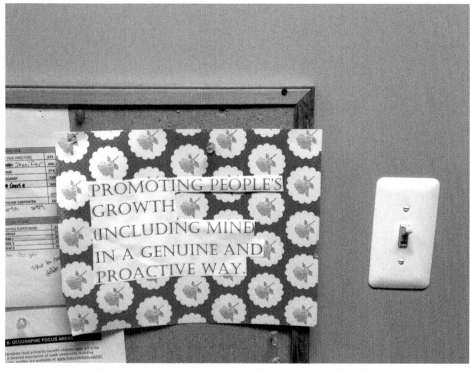

Photo of a mission statement on the wall at Macomb Family Services.

and grow so that we can help more people. That larger, collective mission is possible only when team members are engaged in self-learning and individual growth, thereby sparking ideas for program improvements and coming up with fresh insights for creating the best environment for ongoing development.

To prepare our personal mission statements, I originally set aside time during our staff retreat to draft these texts. Then, months later, we had the statements printed out in colorful ways and we reflected on them, again, in a second session. In this book's pages we will share our basic approach to creating these texts. We are aware that a lot has been published online—from many different professional perspectives—about the process of creating personal mission statements. Feel free to use this section of our book as your guide through the process—or you may want to search for more ideas online and blend them with our practices, to create your own unique workshop or retreat.

I began our process by facilitating a discussion around the passion of our collective work, then asking the group to spend about 15 minutes with paper and pen, sitting quietly somewhere and listing personal accomplishments that continue to be a source of pride. I relayed: "Quickly jot down things you have accomplished in your life that you still remember to this day. You're recalling things you did that make you feel good when you remember them. You can call this a sense of pride, or a warm feeling or a pleasant memory of something you accomplished. Whatever wording you use, your goal is a list of accomplishments, large and small, that are encouraging for you to remember. Don't write about each one at great length. Just try to remember and jot down a list that fits this description."

Then, as people began to look as though they were finished with this task, I called: "Time!"

Next, I asked them to silently read back over the lists they had made. "Can you draw connective lines between items you've listed? Take a few more minutes, now, to do this. You'll be thinking about how the accomplishments you've noted on your paper connect with each other. Is there a central pathway among the memories that are surfacing? Draw lines on your paper, if that helps. Circle things. Jot down some words that describe the pathways you see that connect what you've remembered."

Then, I said: "Please take a fresh sheet of paper. Now I'm going to ask you to list some of the values that you consider essential in your life. Don't get hung up on what the word 'value' means. There are many definitions of value in various academic disciplines. You probably can best answer this question by simply using your own first impression of the phrase '*my* values.' Another way to think about this step is to ask yourself this question: 'What are the underlying truths—your basic assumptions about life—that help you to navigate through each day?'"

If you are working with professionals from many disciplines, you can wind up in a deep discussion of terms like values and ideals. Participants may even bring up tangential themes, ranging from spirituality to politics. Sociologist Wayne Baker, who wrote this book's preface, has spent years studying American values and concludes that the vast majority of Americans share a surprising number of common values. Here are just five of the nearly universal American values, as Baker describes them, based on his research:

- Respect for others: acceptance and appreciation of people of different racial, ethnic and religious groups
- Self-reliance and individualism: reliance on oneself; independence; emphasis on individual strengths and accomplishments
- Equal opportunity: equal access to jobs, education, voting, etc. regardless of age, gender, race, or other factors; a level playing field
- Pursuit of happiness: enjoyment, leisure, pleasure
- Justice and fairness: all the world's people should live in harmony; justice and fairness for all, even people we don't know

Baker lists more American core values in his book, *United America*. Because nearly 9 out of 10 Americans share these core values, you may find your participants using phrases that touch on these themes. Or, you may find that people jot down references to their spiritual life or they may jot down metaphors for core values. What are metaphors for values?

In his most famous speech, "I Have a Dream," Dr. Martin Luther King, Jr. listed many metaphors for American values. This is a complex subject and you may want to further explore the question of values in a future staff workshop or retreat. But, in trying to complete personal mission statements, I would advise keeping this step in the workshop fairly simple. I like focusing participants on the basic question: "What are the underlying truths—your basic values or assumptions about life—that help you to navigate through each day?" That question also keeps us focused on the theme of finding a meaningful path that we hope to follow as individuals and, eventually, as a cooperative team.

You could give your team members another 10 minutes to think about this question of values, and make notes. But observe your participants. If they are deeply engaged in the task, give them plenty of time. If they become restless at some point, you could end this process sooner. Some may enjoy this; some may resist it. Some people are empowered by this kind of reflection; other people think on a more concrete level and find this frustrating. When participants are finished, their notes about values may look very similar—or they may reflect diverse responses to the question. Either way, the exercise is valuable.

When the participants' individual values lists are complete, move on to the final step in creating a mission statement. At this point you could say something like, "Three questions we face every day are: 'Who do I want to be?' 'Why am I doing what I am doing?' and 'How can I best accomplish this?'. Now that you know for yourself what, why, and how you can begin distilling your reflections into a mission statement.

For example, you could say to your group: "This is all about charting our pathway through a typical day. Earlier, we made connections between accomplishments that light up our lives—accomplishments that make us feel good, or warm, or proud. We looked for pathways linking those positive memories. Then, we thought about this on a much higher level. What are the core values that help us walk our pathways every day? Now it's time to distill those insights into a couple of sentences. Now we're going to actually draft our personal mission statements. Don't write too much. When we're done, we'll plan to keep these personal mission statements handy, so they need to be fairly short. We hope to say to each other: 'Here's what I think I'm all about these days. At my best, here's what defines a good day for me.' We're going to ask each other: 'Will you hold me to what I've just written?'"

Make your own judgment about how long your team members should work on their final statements. Depending on the dynamics of your gathering, you might want to take a break after the statements are drafted—then, after the break, ask your team members to revisit their statements. They may want to tweak a few phrases at that time.

Finally, ask participants to read their statements aloud. You could structure this reflective part of the day toward the end of your time together, and have participants depart with these positive affirmations in mind. Or, alternatively, you may want to couple your sharing of the statements with a strength-based discussion. Are participants surprised at how much they share? Are there distinctive differences? How might individual mission statements fit together to form a shared pathway? How can individual strengths build a healthier community?

The personal mission statements are likely to be diverse in their tone and format. Here are a few examples from our team:

- To provide a supportive, peaceful environment so that everyone can grow, feel hope, and have the tools they need to provide quality, meaningful services to the community.
- I build strong relationships that move change in my community. I stir up passion. I create a safe place. I spark a fire. I honor my commitments. I believe in quality. What I do every day makes a difference in a child's life.
- Promoting people's growth, including mine, in a genuine and proactive way.
- I provide quality service by being friendly and compassionate to the people I come in contact with every day and hold true to my word when I say I'll do something.
- To assist, model, and provide support to caregivers and parents with information and resources on age-appropriate practices for young children as they develop skills for kindergarten.
- I strive to live a balanced life and be the best version of myself every day. I give of myself unconditionally while promoting positivity and fairness. I lead those with a need for motivation or inspiration and follow when I recognize my own need for guidance.
- To join with others to promote positive changes in life circumstances.

At Macomb Family Services, we held a second session of reflection on our mission statements a few months after the first session. Before that second experience, a team member volunteered to print out all of our statements on 8-by-11 sheets of paper with decorative borders. Together, we revisited what we had written earlier.

This process was so meaningful to staff that they decided to hang their mission statements on the wall near our desks as both individual affirmations and pledges that we will hold each other accountable. We want to travel a shared pathway, drawing on all of the gifts, talents and passions that light up the lives of our team members—and the clients we serve.

Why Do Relationships
Matter So Much?

From Christine Zimmerman

Why do relationships matter? It's a fair question. If your team is comprised of capable professionals, then you may be asking questions like: "Why can't each individual be responsible for his or her own work, and avoid time-consuming interaction with other people? Isn't that more efficient?" We are all aware of management strategies that rely on competition and incentives that encourage individual achievement and advancement. So why spend time building healthy relationships?

In our organization, we believe in a widely quoted African proverb: "If you want to travel fast, travel alone. If you want to travel far, travel together."

We can all point to organizations in which strong, competitive individuals seem to quickly and efficiently meet their goals—and win accolades, promotions and often financial rewards, as well. However, we see our daily mission—as individuals and as a team—through a different lens. We aren't trying to quickly score a "win" as individuals; we are trying to build a healthier, more sustainable community in our region of Michigan. That longer pathway is full of surprises, pitfalls, roadblocks and counter-productive temptations—but ahead of us is the ultimate reward of strengthening the entire community. Even after we turn off the lights and head home each evening, we know that our corner of the country is a little bit better for everyone because of the work we have done as individuals. By collaborating with others on this larger goal, we end up with something much greater than we could have imagined if we had traveled this pathway as individuals.

In our field of expertise, research confirms a link between the strength of professional relationships and the range of positive program outcomes, for the adults who are the caregivers—parents and teachers—as well as for their children. A search of professional literature will turn up a range of studies over the last decade that reflect this. This may be true in your field of expertise, as well. We strongly believe in following the best practices that continue to emerge among experts in our field of work. We participate in the rigorous analysis of data that we collect to evaluate the overall effectiveness of our programs. As we write this book, we are proud that current analysis is demonstrating our effectiveness in the programs supported by the Social Innovation Fund. We strongly support the use of proven analytic tools. For example, we measure changes in children using a social-emotional assessment tool called the Devereux Early Childhood Assessment (DECA). Data analysis helps us to demonstrate that we are, indeed, achieving our goals. Solid analysis also helps us to zero in on the most important aspects of our current work—and it helps us to drive the direction of our team in the future.

However, an analysis of data only tells part of the story. Agencies and employees can get caught up in outcomes and miss some of the intangible results that occur during our work with clients. Our data-driven analysis may miss the deeper and longer-lasting changes that we are sparking within the community. Data reports can miss the details that fall outside the scope of our current analysis—like interactions with members of our community on a regular basis that can lead to new developments in our overall work.

Early one morning, I was alone at our office, working at my desk. The office doorbell rang, and coming to visit us was a mom from one of our Play and Learn groups, with a loaf of banana bread in her hands. "I appreciate so much how welcoming and supportive everyone is," she told me, as she presented her gift. "So, I made this fresh banana bread for you to share—to say thanks to all of you."

I still remember her visit—especially her use of the word "everyone" and her approach to preparing and offering this small gift. She understood that we are a team—and that we work through a network of relationships with men, women and children in our community. Her words, and the simple gift of bread, told me that she understood our approach to this work.

She brought more than bread that day. She also had three bags of mulch that she was donating for flowers that had been planted by families during a Play and Learn session the week before. And that's not the end of the story. Later that day, I learned that this same mom was reaching out and offering support to another member of her Play and Learn group—a mom who was new to the group. This newcomer had two young children and a husband in the military who had just been deployed. Parents in that Play and Learn group prepared homemade meals, then froze them and delivered them to this mother who suddenly was caring for her children without her husband in the home. "When you're having a hard day, pull one of these out of the freezer," this mother was told, as the frozen dinners were delivered.

These are common experiences for us. What this mom did clearly meets our larger goal of building a healthier community for everyone—both parents and children included. We strive to be an agency that fosters the feeling of good will and community that this mom demonstrates. We see actions like that as something we would like to foster on many levels. But these are not results that will be picked up in data analysis, because this woman's several forms of contribution were unexpected and fell beyond the scope of our regular programming—though her actions certainly help to explain our positive effectiveness.

This mom was paying it forward—a value we encourage in the relationships we build—or, as Dr. Wayne Baker would describe it, this mom was demonstrating *generalized reciprocity*. We're helping each other because it's a good thing to do, without any specific expectation of a return on our investment of time, energy and friendship. We pay it forward—and we encourage others to do the same—because we know that our whole community is stronger if we all act this way.

When a professional or an agency focuses only on funder outcomes, they can often miss important relationships that could impact and expand their work. If they are looking only for immediate benefit to themselves, and their vision is limited to a specific list of goals in front of them, than they could miss the possibility of fostering rich relationships that might prompt future opportunities.

When a facilitator from our agency takes our Play and Learn programming to a new location within the community—such as a school where we have not worked before—we understand that we are bringing more than a request for space for our activities. We welcome the potential for new partnerships to form because of our arrival. In contrast, a professional focused on individual goal achievement could simply contact the administrator of a site, such as a principal, get permission to use a classroom, and then show up each week to facilitate a Play and Learn group. Data likely will show that this individual has met expected outcomes in the group—and the experience might be judged a success. But that isn't enough for us. Instead, our team encourages facilitators to take a longer path, spending the time it takes to encourage collaboration as our program is expanding. We intentionally talk with administrative staff not just once, to secure permission, but whenever we enter the building. If our host site is a school, we foster relationships with the teachers who seem interested in our work. As a result, many teachers now ask us for support as they work with children and encounter situations in which they could use some of our expertise and counsel. Because these teachers are aware of the positive effects of our work, they understand the impact our facilitators can have on families, and they encourage parents to use our services— groups, workshops and other training classes. This not only helps our program to expand, but it also enriches the quality of our work with families when we are coordinating in a friendly and cooperative way with the other professionals.

Another example of a professional opportunity often disregarded by organizations with a narrower view of their mission is open houses. In our field, these events crop up every year. A school or other community center organizes an open house and invites representatives from a wide range of nonprofits to set up tables, bring materials to share and then talk with open-house visitors. These events generally don't produce a large number of new enrollments, so some groups ignore them. Within our team, however, we have no problem finding volunteers to represent Macomb Family Services at local open houses. That's because we understand the larger benefit of participating. Beyond trying to sign up interested visitors, open houses are important professional networking opportunities. Our team members learn a lot about the wide range of other services our clients could receive in our area of Michigan. And usually, we discover new resources not currently provided through our agency, so we return from an open house with a much greater awareness of the many ways we can collectively help caregivers, parents and children. Judged on the basis of enrollment numbers, open houses can seem like a waste of time. But we are looking for a much broader range of possibilities when building relationships.

One more example of a frequently missed opportunity lies in the way regional nonprofits and agencies tend to staff collaborative gatherings. Across the country, many professional groups hold such regional sessions on a regular basis. But some nonprofits or agencies tend to send a different staffer to each meeting, as if such opportunities to collaborate are merely bureaucratic assignments and regular participation does not matter. I have seen groups that handle such assignments as a kind of short-straw rotating requirement, as some staffer just shows up and logs the hours in the group. Usually, these one-time representatives tend to fade into the background. Perfunctory attendance signals disengagement and a loss of opportunity for deeper community involvement. In contrast, regular participants get to know one another. They learn about the diversity of regional programs—and about the people who run those programs.

Organize Your Own Road to Relationships Retreat

From Christine Zimmerman

If you liked our ideas on using personal mission statements in team building, then consider organizing a workshop or retreat around the benefits, pitfalls and temptations that can prevent building good relationships—and then, encouraging what we describe as Signature Strengths that you can promote in your team as you build a healthier community.

Many resources and significant research on healthy relationships can be found online, including in recent journal articles and books. For general readers, several of Robert J. Wicks' books contain detailed tips and checklists for healthy relationships, as well as for resiliency among caregivers. His 2010 book, *Bounce: Living the Resilient Life* (Oxford Press), is designed for individual reflection as well as workshops, and includes a six-page Questionnaire on Personal Strengths and Virtues that can be easily adapted for a retreat.

Use our ideas in this book; gather more online; borrow ideas from books—and organize your own retreat. In our book, we are contributing to this growing body of resources for encouraging stronger professional relationships. Based on our experiences, we have created a five-page drawing describing our road to relationships. Feel free to use these colorful pages to spark your own discussions. The comic panels are almost self-explanatory and are fancifully designed to prompt smiles and creativity. The first page introduces our approach to personal mission statements. The next four pages encourage participants to discuss the following:

- Who will travel with you? As we say on that page of the comic: "Everyone brings talents." The comic character opens a treasure chest and asks, "What are your talents?" In your workshop or retreat, spend time talking about the relationships you hope to encourage. Are you considering a diversity of skills, of socioeconomic backgrounds, of ethnicity, of ages? Remember Kathleen Macdonald's example of the phoropter. Are you considering this question through different lenses? Who might we want to invite on the journey with us?

- Pitfalls! For this portion, we have drawn together a list of real dangers that people encounter as they reach out to form new relationships—especially among professionals who are bridging various disciplines and agencies. We suggest on that page that your group identify a more specific list of potential pitfalls. Be honest about your own fears in your own community! Take a look at your agency culture; is it gossipy or competitive? Sometimes we are tempted by pitfalls that can masquerade as good intentions such as insults in the guise of venting or sarcasm in the guise of humor, but others may wind up nursing unintentional wounds. These sometimes subtle shortcomings can waylay even the most highly motivated professionals: among overworked professionals, a common pitfall is falling into discouragement and apathy. That dual temptation is addressed in many of Robert Wicks' books, as he encourages resiliency. Self-reflection needs to be fostered in an intentional way to increase awareness and make it easier to avoid such pitfalls.

- Collaboration. We take our "strength-based approach" very seriously in all aspects of our work. So, while it is important to name and discuss potential dangers, fears and temptations, we also recommend that you include, in your workshop or retreat, a rich discussion of the values that contribute to collaboration. In the next comic panel, our team shows those values blossoming along our Road to Relationships. Discussing these values—and then asking your staff to add their own phrases to the list—will encourage a collective mindfulness about behaviors that will wind up strengthening the entire team.

■ Signature Strengths! Finally, we encourage you to wrap up your journey down our Road to Relationships by listing your group's Signature Strengths.

Signature Strengths

From Christine Zimmerman

Don't take our word for it! Don't simply accept our list of Signature Strengths in the final panel of the comic. We're simply offering suggestions. Your group should discuss and list strengths that you collectively hope will become hallmarks of your own teamwork. You might find it helpful to draw connective lines—or you might describe it more creatively, as "sketching your pathway" and reaching all the way back to your team's set of personal mission statements. The ultimate goal is an honest, unified sense of mission and an awareness that distinctive, individual talents can be shared and celebrated by the entire team. So as you reach the conclusion of this process, you'll find it helpful to spend time reflecting on your own group's list of Signature Strengths. It's another way to help define a collective, collaborative vision, as you bring your talents together to serve your community.

Here are six Signature Strengths that our Macomb Family Services team strives to embody in its work:

1. **Elevating others**. Call this "paying it forward" or "generalized reciprocity," or use another phrase you prefer. Elevating others is central to our work and our relationships.

   We always start by elevating, or supporting, our team members and then, by extension, we collectively lift up our larger community and our entire region of Michigan. Claiming this Signature Strength requires a lot of personal awareness among our team members. For example, we know that we can't simply show up at a meeting with a personal agenda, and then push our own ideas without inviting contributions. The longer path that we take involves facilitating the resourcefulness of group members. Time after time, we find that fully involving people with differing values, beliefs and talents supports our collective growth. Yes, it can be a frustrating process, and sometimes, it can require more time than it would if we simply allowed one strong member of the group to make policies and issue edicts. But, ultimately, we serve a diverse community, and we find that elevating others means that our collaborative ideas usually are more effective than any one participant's preconceived agenda would have been.

We consistently practice disciplined listening and questioning, as well as a withholding of judgment until a consensus is emerging. We encourage the values of curiosity and fairness and encouragement. That's part of our strength-based approach to our work at all levels. If this idea of elevating others interests you, you will find many other resources on collaborative decision-making in journals and books. It may not be an easy process to implement. It's not a strength that a group can quickly claim, vote to enact and then assume that everyone authentically shares. There are many challenges to truly embracing a culture that elevates others. One big challenge concerns vulnerability, which we claim as our second Signature Strength.

2. **Vulnerability**. I am the director of our programs, but I'm usually not the smartest person in the room. If you are a community leader, have you ever found yourself admitting this? It's just one way to think about vulnerability as a strength. Is this an uncomfortable admission for you to make? Well, pause to think about this issue for a moment, and it starts to make a lot of sense in an era when people carry super-powered computers in their pockets—aka their smartphones. Even if you are a highly trained professional with years of service behind you, the potential of misstating facts (easily checked by your audience on their phones) or missing the latest news (just a few taps away on those phones) can be a humbling experience. Extend that awareness of your vulnerability to include an appreciation of the rich array of talents embodied in the lives of your

team members and you can begin to appreciate the value of a healthy vulnerability.

I tend to start our planning meetings with questions like, "What are some of the goals we want to achieve with this project?" Then I help our group find clarity within our objectives. We often quickly settle on effective courses of action, with enthusiastic participation by team members.

It's true, though, that building relationships around a value such as vulnerability takes time and may be difficult for some personalities to accept. It's one of our Signature Strengths, but we know it is often challenging to live by. One complementary value that can help you to attain a healthy vulnerability is our next Signature Strength: engagement.

3. **Engagement**. Merriam-Webster tells us that engagement is "emotional involvement or commitment." We might also describe it as "responsiveness," and it is closely related to "empathy." In plain language, at Macomb Family Services, we truly care about one another.

It's easy to claim this strength; it's difficult to embody it. Healthy relationships can't grow in a culture of impersonal interactions—or, worse, in a culture of dog-eat-dog competition. Real engagement takes work. There are many disciplines you can practice in order to deepen the engagement of your team members. For example, an engaged person pays attention to subtle messages given in many forms of expression—often unspoken or unwritten—as well as to the direct messages we typically voice or write. An engaged person is fully aware of other people. Does that sound easy? How often do you find yourself texting or checking social media on your phone during a collaborative meeting? How often do you find yourself in this scenario: You're multi-tasking at your desk, and not fully engaged with the person on your telephone, the co-worker at the next desk with whom you're supposed to be collaborating, the friend you're messaging on the computer or the other friend you've just emailed?

Real engagement also involves our next Signature Strength: compassion.

4. **Compassion.** A quick way to measure the strength of your compassion is to think about how you respond to anger when it inevitably flares up within an organization or among your clients. We once had an unfortunate experience with an agency that had named a new director, and that process had somehow resulted in a mixed-up list of contacts that was passed along in the transition. The new director had been trying to reach our agency for quite a while, but mistakenly had been calling another group. When one of our team members finally crossed paths with this woman, she was furious! Angrily, she slammed her hand on her desk and yelled, "Where have you been? I've been trying to get help!"

How should we have responded? It wasn't our fault. Returning her fury with anger at the inappropriate outburst would have been a natural response. But if one of your Signature Strengths is compassion, then encountering an angry person sparks a different kind of response. Why was this woman so frustrated? How could we respond in a helpful way? Our first instinct wasn't self-justification; it was concern for this woman who was obviously exasperated.

I'm proud to say that our team member responded with compassion that day. Meeting anger with anger is such an easy temptation! Our staffer chose to listen until she understood what was going on in this frustrating situation. She asked about ways she could help to support this new director. At the end of the conversation, the two women were able to work together on goals that the director felt were important. As a result, we have a solid relationship with this director and her agency in an ongoing way.

In professional relationships, anger is often a naked blade that flashes too quickly in frustrating situations, and thereby makes things worse—when a discipline of compassion could resolve the problem in a positive way.

Another reaction to anger can be withdrawal. Who wants to face a furious person? But withdrawal can lead to disengagement and can contribute to feelings of despair and even apathy, and that centuries-old temptation of acedia, a sense of hopelessness. We've found that compassion can be a potent antidote to these destructive cycles.

Think that compassion is one of your Signature Strengths? Flip the lenses again in your group's phoropter and consider whether you could claim this next strength as well: inclusiveness.

5. **Inclusiveness.** Throughout this book—and in all of our work in southeast Michigan—we are committed to inclusivity. We work with a diverse population of families and community partners that includes various backgrounds, economic status, ethnicity, and value systems. In 2016, Pew Research reported a sense of inclusiveness as an essential part of any fully engaged community work in the United States. According to Pew:

Americans are more racially and ethnically diverse than in the past, and the U.S. is projected to be even more diverse in the coming decades. By 2055, the U.S. will not have a single racial or ethnic majority. Much of this change has been—and will be—driven by immigration. Nearly 59 million immigrants have arrived in the U.S. in the past 50 years, mostly from Latin America and Asia.

What's more, diversity is not merely a matter of ethnicity. Remember the many lenses we can flip in our phoropter to see the world with greater clarity? Pew also reports that diversity is a matter of economic status, gender and also age. At Macomb Family Services we believe that diversity also encompasses various approaches derived from professional and life experiences.

Diversity provides an opportunity for richer collaboration and generates creative ideas. Holding the value of diversity encourages us to include structures in meetings and discussions that allow every voice in the room to be heard. And, finally, we summon all of the strengths that define the culture of our agency and we name this as our final Signature Strength: true partnerships.

6. **True Partnerships.** We list true partnerships as our ultimate Signature Strength. We regard this as the ultimate goal along our Road to Relationships.

   At Macomb Family Services, this value also extends into each contact that we have with teachers, parents and caregivers. We don't arrive on the scene assuming that our experts know all the answers. We are proud of our professional expertise, of course, but we are perpetually forming true partnerships with the people we work with in an ongoing way. The adults we encounter on a daily basis often have a great deal of insight into the lives of their children and a deep reserve of love for these children, as well. Just as we seek to exercise our strengths in peer-to-peer professional relationships, we embody these values as we form true, working partnerships with adults throughout our community.

How can you evaluate your group's openness to this overall idea of a Road to Relationships?

As we close this chapter, consider a final question from our experience: When is the last time you enjoyed a good old-fashioned picnic? We have been talking about workshops and retreats in this section of our book, but we also have discovered the value of interacting with the community through the American tradition of relaxing together and sharing a meal outdoors.

When we decided to organize our first picnic, we invited other local agencies to participate. At first, we were disappointed to find that many of our invitations were declined. The managers couldn't see how this idea related to their groups' anticipated outcomes. But we held the picnic anyway. And we've been doing it year after year since.

Today, that picnic is a wonderful, widely anticipated annual event. Attendance has grown every year. We keep it very simple and we've seen many unexpected benefits. It is a time when families, teachers and staff can join together and have some fun at no cost. This has also become a way for other family members (especially fathers and grandparents) to attend and become engaged in our programming in an emotionally safe and fun way.

Together, we're building a healthier community!

Our
Recommendations

From the Michigan League for Public Policy.

Are you inspired by the stories you read in this book? Do you know that you can help to bring such experiences to your community? You can help yourself and other parents—as well as teachers and caregivers—by increasing awareness of these issues in your part of the country.

This chapter of our book is a compilation of recommendations from several sources including one of Michigan's top experts Alicia Guevara Warren, the Michigan League for Public Policy's project director for Kids Count in Michigan.

The biggest challenge in affecting public policy is that social-emotional development is often discounted, because it's harder to demonstrate change in this area when it is compared with preschool programs that help children to name their letters and to count.

If you are inspired to take action, you will find that legislators at every level are approached by a lot of people promoting many important issues, and they have very demanding schedules. It's often best to approach your local legislators first.

How can you connect most effectively? Learn about the legislative calendar in your region. In Michigan, November is usually when budget discussions start for the following fiscal year. It is usually easier to approach legislators for small pilot projects and then—after positive results are shown—chances increase for sustained funding. It is also helpful to identify legislators whose priorities are in alignment with the work you are promoting. Not everyone will be interested or have a background in your area of concern, so the best way to start is by researching an individual whom you plan to approach. Websites describing lawmakers' bios and backgrounds will help you find those personal connections. For example, you might find that a legislator's spouse is an early childhood preschool teacher, so that becomes a common denominator. Legislators with young children themselves may identify more readily with early childhood issues, and therefore might be easier to engage.

Legislators are very busy, so you have to make your time count when meeting with them. You might only get about 15 minutes, or you might wind up first meeting with a member of the legislator's staff. Come prepared to be concise and then convey your message simply and quickly. Keeping this in mind, consider creating a one- or two-sided infographic or fact sheet. The piece should briefly explain the program you're bringing to their attention, highlight what the data is showing, and include a clear "ask" that explains what is needed from them (i.e., funding in the budget for a specific program, a yes or no vote on a specific bill, etc.).

Don't be disappointed if you start by meeting with a member of the staff. The policy and legislative staff who support a legislator are important to build relationships with as well. They are often the gatekeepers to the legislator, determining what ends up on the legislator's desk or schedule. If you can earn the support of the staff, they, in turn, can often facilitate your connection with the legislator.

It is important to develop different materials for different audiences. The staff will typically want more in-depth materials to dig into and learn more from; executive summaries or infographics will help distill things for their bosses.

Developing relationships is key and has to occur over time. Legislators see a lot of people and groups—especially if they schedule "advocacy days"—and most of these visitors never see the legislator or the staff twice. Make sure that you continue to build your relationships and follow up over time. Don't just leave a meeting and assume you are finished. Send a thank-you note for their time. Find out about any coffee hours or town hall meetings that are scheduled in the future. Visit the legislator's website and sign up for email newsletters that are relevant. It's important to be patient and persistent. Change will not happen immediately.

Relationships are a two-way street. Don't just approach legislators with your request—become a constant resource for them. Give them data and information about the program you support. Statistics help give our issues backbone and show that these matters shouldn't be subjective or partisan. If you come across an article that would be helpful in understanding your issue of interest, send it to your legislators and the staff. It's a good idea to include a short note like, "I thought this might be helpful to you." Send them notices of events coming up where they could learn more about the issues that matter to you. Invite them to come to a site visit.

The more connections and concise, helpful communication you share, the better. Depending on the issue or the event, a legislator or a staff member will often try to visit. Building relationships with the staff through this kind of helpful follow-up visit is equally important, especially when you can become a beneficial resource to them in return. Staff members often have inside insight and information that is extremely valuable.

In Michigan, there is already a lot of support for early childhood issues. However, this primarily takes the form of general support—and how that support develops in a policy context can be vastly different over time. Think carefully about ways you can help lawmakers and administrators of public agencies understand the specific issues and policies that most concern you. A well-intentioned legislator may assume that the only early childhood issue that matters is whether a parent can find a preschool for a 4-year-old child. Especially after reading this book, you may be inspired to help develop programs for a wider age range—or you may want to highlight the need for classes and consulting in regards to social-emotional issues. There are many factors that contribute to a child's well-being, and this should be communicated to legislators—and demonstrated with data and real stories about the experiences of children and their families.

Personal stories are always the most powerful, so think about how you can collect and report data to broaden those stories to show powerful trends or perhaps emerging challenges in your community. As you consider how to use any time you may be able to schedule with legislators in your region, also think about people whom you may want to have accompany you. For policymakers, it's helpful to hear from families who can describe some of their challenges—especially people from the legislator's own district. Of course, carefully plan what you and your companions will say and organize your time so that you cover everything you had hoped to convey in the precious minutes you'll be given.

Finally, in many parts of the United States, term limits now mean that there are regular opportunities for community leaders to step up, plan a campaign and fill legislative offices. It's a mixed blessing. If you do build a solid relationship with a representative or senator, a term limit may sideline that official after a couple of years. On the other hand, if you already are a community leader in your part of the U.S., then you may know someone who is planning to run for office in the future. That is yet another opportunity to form valuable relationships to promote more effective early childhood resources. If you find yourself frustrated with current legislators, remember that you may be just a year or two away from a term limit. Perhaps, if you are becoming a well-known advocate, you may choose to run for an office yourself.

Politics and public advocacy are challenging, aren't they? Of course! This work is tough and it's easy to lose hope. But be persistent. This is challenging work. It takes time and constant engagement.

As you read our book, you may find yourself unable to take on such active roles. Remember that most legislators—and heads of public agencies—can cite true stories of laws, policies and funding priorities that changed after a single transformative experience. In some cases, constituents' thought-provoking telephone calls or pieces published in local newspapers wind up making a significant difference. Do you know what publications your legislators follow? Have you considered placing a thoughtful telephone call? Media interest and political interest often go hand-in-hand, so it's important to keep that avenue of advocacy in mind as well.

In these few pages, we've tried to offer an overview of effective advocacy. In your part of the U.S., it is likely that you will find nonprofits willing to help you fine-tune your efforts on whatever issue is closest to your heart. Finally, here are a few thoughts from Gilda Z. Jacobs, president and CEO of the Michigan League for Public Policy:

> Advocacy is about taking our collective knowledge and passion and putting it to work to create a better Michigan for all. There are a few simple tips for effective advocacy: Be patient and resilient, even though results are slow to come; stay true to your mission, but also be adaptable; and be targeted and focus on the minds and votes you can actually change. Remember to always localize and personalize your issue, and praise as much as you criticize; but hold policymakers accountable for their actions. Finally, don't stop doing what you're doing. The people of Michigan need you. You have to stay engaged to help ensure that legislators are, too.

*The **Michigan League for Public Policy (MLPP)** is a nonpartisan policy institute focused on economic opportunity for all. It is the only state-level organization that addresses poverty in a comprehensive way. If you are interested in learning more about the League, please visit* www. mlpp.org, *sign up to receive our monthly e-newsletter and follow us on social media.*

Our Partners

Why this matters so much to us

From Dr. Herman B. Gray, M.D., MBA, President and
CEO of United Way for Southeastern Michigan:

As the father of two thriving adult children, I fully understand
the challenges of parenting. Even under the best of circumstances, parenting is the most difficult, and yet fulfilling, duty that
many of us will face.

My wife, Shirley, and I had it pretty easy with our two girls,
but of course, there were always challenges. Homework time
was a battleground as the girls struggled with math. These were
moments that tested me. (They also proved that I would've made
a terribly impatient tutor.) And like many parents, we dealt with
stubbornness from our youngest, who pronounced "I know that"
to everything that came her way, whether she truly did or not.

I wasn't alone in these moments. As a pediatrician, I saw that
the parents of my young patients shared the same worries as me,
and I sympathized with them. They would often ask questions
like:

"Will they get into the 'right' school?"

"Will they be happy?"

"Will they make a good living?"

My role was to offer nonjudgmental support, accurate advice
and reassurance. Perhaps one of the greatest parenting challenges is helping our children develop good judgment, moral
character and intellectual strength.

It is a tough business raising a child.

Whether a child is 6 or 60, parenting never truly ends, but I
am proud to say that both of my girls graduated from the University of Michigan—one earning a master's degree and another

a law degree. It makes me proud to see my children passionately pursuing and leading in their careers.

Every child deserves the opportunity to succeed, and it is our collective responsibility to support them. That is why our Social Innovation Fund work is so important. It's structured to create best-in-class practices to help parents and caregivers access the resources and tools needed to support the children in their lives. This work has the potential to not only affect our local community, but it can influence nationwide policy as well.

If we do not move forward to meet the challenges of our ever-changing world, we will fall behind. We cannot be afraid to try new or different approaches to age-old social conditions. Our community's success depends on how we care for and develop our children, which is why it is crucial that we work together and use creative strategies to prepare them for a global future.

My work at United Way for Southeastern Michigan (UWSEM) means a great deal to me. I am fully committed to the service of others and to making the world our children live in a better place. We can only carry out this work with our dedicated partners and with the support of our community, and I am grateful for the opportunity we have to collaborate with and learn from one another.

At United Way, we embrace our legacy as leaders in social innovation, and we move forward confidently into an unknown future, growing and learning, and always serving. I hope the books in *The Bib to Backpack Learning Series* will help to guide many parents and community leaders in how we might achieve our goals together – and create a brighter future for our children.

Herman Gray, M.D., MBA, is president and CEO of United Way for Southeastern Michigan, appointed to his current post in 2015. Before that, he served as the executive vice president of pediatric health services at the Detroit Medical Center (DMC); prior, he was the DMC Children's Hospital of Michigan's president and chief executive officer for eight years, after serving as its chief operating officer and chief of staff. Dr. Gray's areas of specialty include health care administration, public health, child advocacy and nonprofit management. His medical degree was from the University of Michigan and his Master of Business Administration was from the University of Tennessee. He and his wife, Shirley, have two daughters.

Tip for Success: Five Themes to Stress With Your Potential Supporters

Most nonprofits face the twin challenges of raising funds and recruiting participants. Consider including these themes as you reach out:

1. Innovation — How does your team transform and adapt ideas as you encounter inevitable challenges?

2. Evidence — How do you know your program works? How is your program designed to shift gears on the basis of new evidence?

3. Scale — How can your program expand? How do you expect to flexibly adapt to the challenges you face as you grow?

4. Match — How can you add additional or matching dollars and why will those new funders choose to join your effort?

5. Knowledge Sharing — How are you contributing to the widespread sharing of fresh ideas and best practices?

Adapted from the SIF Communicators Toolkit

Tips from United Way and the Social Innovation Fund

In 2009, the Social Innovation Fund (SIF) was launched through the Corporation for National and Community Service (CNCS), the federal agency that sponsors many service programs, including AmeriCorps, Learn and Serve America and Senior Corps. What made CNCS's new SIF initiative distinctive in the existing array of federal programs was three of its core goals: a commitment to collaborate with already existing nonprofits across the country, rather than creating new federal programs from scratch; a strong mandate to include ongoing collection of data and evaluation of each funded program to demonstrate effectiveness; and a pledge to widely share information that could foster scaling and replication of similarly effective programs. The book you are reading is a major part of United Way for Southeastern Michigan's effort to reach that third goal. The six books in what we are calling *The Bib to Backpack Learning Series* provide transparent and detailed information on how the programs of our six Metro Detroit partners began, how they overcame challenges along the way and how the programs are structured today. The books themselves are easily accessible doorways into our programs — and into the larger potential of the SIF. In addition, by producing high-quality books that share the story of the programs, we also are equipping our six regional nonprofit partners with a valuable tool for their ongoing work with community leaders and funders. Each of these nonprofit groups now can say that they literally are "writing the book" on how to help with early education in challenging neighborhoods through ongoing innovation. That's a major boost in convincing additional partners to support this work.

If you are thinking about developing a program in your region, you also will want to explore the hundreds of pages of tips and detailed analysis of existing programs that are shared by the SIF at http://www.nationalservice.gov/programs/social-innovation-fund/knowledge-initiative/reports. These online SIF materials are free to download in PDF format and are packed with helpful information about strategies that already are working in communities from coast to coast. Since one goal of this fund is to encourage robust sharing of information, you may even discover programs in your region that could collaborate with your group in the future.

If you explore the federal website, you will find details on two programs with similar-sounding names that are administered by CNCS. The original 2009 SIF, which is supporting the six programs in southeast Michigan, is sometimes referred to as "SIF Classic" to distinguish it from a new program that was launched in 2014 that is called "SIF Pay for Success." That newer program changes the funding model to leverage federal money only after other organizations have established a program and have proven that it works. The Detroit-area programs are part of the original SIF — but, at this point, either fund may interest community leaders in your part of the country. Both are covered on the federal website.

The following helpful ideas are paraphrased from several public reports, including a late-2015 analysis called *State of the SIF Report*, the *SIF Communicators Toolkit* and a *Lessons and Stories* report, focused on United Way.

Question: Has your involvement with the SIF, including the evaluation component, helped you when meeting with funders?

Answer from UWSEM: Education and youth development is a major focus in our region, and funders also understand the value of SIF. The quality of the SIF's mandated evaluations are especially appealing to many funders who are now expecting to see increased levels of accountability tied to their funds. The national prominence of the SIF, coupled with the fact that this connects with a major focus in our region, has allowed our fund development teams to feel comfortable approaching both funders we work with consistently as well as establishing new relationships with groups that want to contribute to the well-being of children and families in our region.

Question: How has your involvement with the SIF enabled your organization to scale your programs?

Answer from UWSEM: We are continuing to work on scaling efforts with our six programs, including the program that is the subject of this book: ACCESS to School. We work with our six organizations in a collaborative way to set scaling and replication goals and to design action plans to reach those goals. We provide each organization with additional staff hours and technical assistance. In 2016, our major effort toward this goal is the creation of this series of six books that will help community leaders nationwide understand how they could replicate these programs. We are also committed to spreading the use of the valuable Ages and Stages Questionnaire through our BibToBackpack.org website. Plus, we continue to gather new data that help us to identify additional communities in need of these early childhood interventions. That will guide the future placement of resources from our current programs.

Question: When telling the story of an organization's current work and its goals in the future, who should be addressed on a regular basis?

Answer from the SIF: Most organizations maintain a list of "target audiences" as they communicate about their work. Take a look at your list to see if it includes:

- Board members – These leaders set the overall direction of your organization and secure ongoing funding. Members of your board need to understand your work and need to know key details they can share as ambassadors for your program.

- Private funders – Your relationship with your funders doesn't end when the money is provided. These funders are gateways to future funding and they need to know that their money is supporting effective, ongoing work.

- Elected officials – These community leaders can help you overcome barriers and, at some levels of government, may be able to appropriate future funding. Consider scheduling a reception or special program to give elected officials an opportunity to understand your work.

- Program beneficiaries and stakeholders – These men and women embody your impact in the community, but they may not understand the full scope of what you are accomplishing if you don't tell them. Also, help them to understand their ongoing role in telling your group's story.

- Social sector influencers – Are you regularly reaching out to academic institutions, other nonprofit organizations, for-profit social enterprises and other thought leaders in your community? Do you know local journalists and media personalities with an interest in your core community? Many groups overlook valuable contacts with these influential individuals and institutions, partly because you may not be updating and expanding your list of contacts on a regular basis.

Four Tips for Communicating With Your Community

1. Communicate regularly – Many organizations are so busy running their programs that they forget there is a larger community that wants to support what they are doing. Consider updates through social media, a monthly newsletter or some other form of ongoing communication.

2. Focus on real people – The strongest public response to your work will come when people see the difference your program makes in the lives of the men, women and children involved. This book is an example of offering human stories as a doorway through which people can explore what you are doing.

3. Share information – Expand the boundaries of your "external communication" to include opportunities for your team to meet with teams from other similar groups. Share innovations and insights.

4. Get creative – Many lengthy reports are generated in a huge program like the SIF. These are essential to track and analyze our evidence, but we also need to find creative, compelling formats for sharing our stories. This series of books is an experiment in sharing of our stories with the world.

Adapted from the SIF Communicators Toolkit

Why United Way is an effective partner

Wherever you are in the world, as you read this book, consider inquiring about the international network of United Way affiliates as a starting point in your efforts to launch a program.

For almost 130 years, United Way affiliates have been leaders in charitable giving focused on meeting pressing community needs in the United States and beyond. Tracing its founding to 1887 in Denver, Colorado, these emerging regional programs bore many names, including Community Chest, a phrase familiar to fans of the classic board game, Monopoly.

A major center in the history of United Way innovation was Detroit, following World War II. That's when financial expert Walter C. Laidlaw adapted lessons from his work with World War II war chest drives to begin building a wide-reaching community consensus that was described in the slogan, "Give Once for All." Laidlaw's reach spanned all levels of the community. For example, he drew avid support from both automotive titan Henry Ford II and pioneering labor leader Walter Reuther. In 1968, Laidlaw retired from his influential role in the organization, and by the 1970s, the phrase "United Way" was becoming widely adopted by the semi-independent affiliates in this worldwide network.

In the late 1980s, criticism arose concerning the way funds were being used in a number of the huge network's American affiliates. At the same time, United Way was facing declines in the automatic donations that had been provided by employees of large corporations since after World War II. As SIF publications describe United Way's history, the organization's 2007 commitment to a new "Community Impact Agenda" was a game-changer in the wake of these problems that had surfaced. One SIF report describes that 2007 change in focus as, "a vision for how United Ways could rebuild trust and remain credible, relevant, and effective." The SIF's analysis continues: "In this vision, United Way affiliates would target a limited number of issues and basic needs whose existence or lack thereof causes or contributes to poverty in communities across the country: income, education, and health. They would look beyond themselves and their network to partner with other grant makers, government agencies, corporations, and nonprofits to concentrate and magnify collective action and investment to tackle difficult social problems."

That's why SIF reports indicate that United Way organizations have proven to be effective partners in this kind of innovative, collaborative program. One SIF report describes the new United Way thinking this way: "United Way would no longer simply write checks to charities and hope they would do what they said they would do; rather, United Way would engage with recipients to strengthen their capacity to implement strong programs. These relationships would move beyond transactional to be transformational." As a result, since 2010, the SIF has funded work through United Way affiliates in parts of Louisiana, Minnesota, Colorado, Ohio, South Carolina, Oregon and Michigan.

However, as anyone who has worked in the nonprofit sector knows, not all grants are immediately accepted. United Way for Southeastern Michigan began its efforts to receive SIF funding in 2010, but had to retool its application before successfully applying in 2011. If you are considering applying for grants, remember that it takes time, sometimes a period measured in years, and you may need to make repeated attempts, even with a first-rate organization supporting your work.

Overall, the benefits of this partnership have been substantial. A SIF *Lessons and Stories* report describes the impact on the Metro Detroit organization this way:

> The SIF experience had transformative impacts on United Way for Southeastern Michigan (UWSEM) and its sub-grantees. It changed how UWSEM selects grantees, fostered a culture of data-informed decision-making, and bolstered formal and informal knowledge sharing.
>
> "SIF has had both direct and indirect impacts on the way that education work is being done here," said

Jennifer Callans, UWSEM's early education director. "The difference between our work before SIF and after is like night and day." ...

UWSEM needed to adapt to the SIF's rigorous evaluation requirements by building capacity for itself and for its sub-grantees in key areas such as data management. UWSEM also needed to align the evaluation activities of its sub-grantees, each of which had its own evaluation plan, third-party evaluator, and data system. To aggregate these different efforts, it worked with its sub-grantees and its portfolio evaluator, Child Trends, to create a common set of outcomes and indicators to serve as the basis for tracking progress across all programs.

If you are reading this book in hopes of launching or expanding a program in your community, many connected with the SIF advise that you first take a close look at the way you collect data about your program and then use it to evaluate your work in an ongoing way. Again, from the Metro Detroit section of the *Lessons and Stories* report:

The experience with data collection for the SIF grant was informative for everyone, including the sub-grantees, notes Jeffrey Miles, UWSEM's SIF manager.

Tip for Success: Climb Out of Your Silo
Big organizations like United Way can easily fall into silos. We might be funding an agency for something in education, something in basic needs and something in financial stability. Then, we realize all those United Way program officers need to be talking to each other. We've started convening cross-functional teams to share experiences with particular grantees across the organization.
From Jennifer Callans, UWSEM's early education director, in a SIF report.

Tips from our portfolio evaluator

Child Trends, founded in 1979 and based in Bethesda, Maryland, is a leading nonprofit research organization focused on improving public policies and interventions that serve children and families. Programs funded by the SIF are required to conduct rigorous evaluation of their effectiveness, and one part of that effort at UWSEM was to contract with Child Trends, which would conduct ongoing interviews and analysis. The following tips are paraphrased from an interim report by Child Trends, drawing on extensive interviews with professionals working in the various SIF programs in the Detroit area. Although specifically focused on these programs in Southeast Michigan, these tips may be useful to anyone developing such programs in the future.

- **Clear and timely communication is essential.** Good communication is one key to success. Because UWSEM administers various SIF programs, the individual groups developing these programs depend on UWSEM for clear directions and compliance information, as well as updates. Communication also is important in the other direction – so that individual programs can voice their concerns, questions and challenges. One key step UWSEM took was to mandate a series of regular meetings to share updates and to hear what the participants were learning across the spectrum of these local programs.

- **Balance rigor with feasibility when it comes to evaluation plans for the new programs.** All SIF grants require evaluation plans, because the SIF's practice is to support and, ideally, to replicate programs that have clear evidence of success. At the same time, organizers need to understand how these evaluation activities may shape program implementation, which in turn may affect findings in the evaluation. This is a challenging aspect of participating in such a grant, and the six Detroit-area programs all found that they had to pay a great deal of attention to meeting this goal. Organizations trying to develop such programs should not try to go it alone. They should meet as a team, discuss, research and develop strategies that can lead to best practices in evaluating the programs – while, at the same time, not compromising program implementation.

- **Build or improve capacity for data collection and management.** Nonprofits participating in a program like this vary in their capacity to track and manage data. Some have an established data collection infrastructure; others merely collect demographic and/or attendance data. The wide range of capacity in data management poses a challenge to systematically collecting high-quality data across all of the participating programs. To improve data quality, organizations considering such programs should take a close look at their own data management systems and share ideas for improving the management of data with other participating nonprofits. Again, don't go it alone in trying to determine how you will manage your data, share best practices with other organizations to improve everyone's capacity.

- **Tailor expectations of scaling to each program's stage of development.** Everyone hopes that good ideas will flourish and that effective programs will expand, but scaling depends on a program's stage of development. Whether programs ultimately prove effective or not, the fact is that programs don't all develop at the same rate. Some have greater barriers to overcome, while many programs must iron out a long series of glitches. Programs that are relatively new to an organization or community may need to gain experience before they can take off and have a smooth ride. It's critically important to realize that not all programs, even effective ones, will scale at the same rate.

- **Address ongoing funding challenges through collective problem solving.** Detroit is an example of an urban area with limited resources for funding and many nonprofits competing for dollars. UWSEM recognizes that challenge and helps to facilitate funding opportunities. But, even with the best intentions, such efforts sometimes do not prove fruitful. Raising local funds is one of the toughest challenges in this kind of work. Organizations considering such programs should try to find out how other similar communities are tackling this widespread problem. Sharing advice and opportunities on fundraising leverages collective problem-solving to address this major issue. By collaborating and sharing ideas with other community leaders, you may discover approaches that will help the entire community.

A Macomb Family Services staffer reads about Tucker the Turtle to two of our Play and Learn children.

Acknowledgements

Macomb Family Services is pleased to have shared in our work with the Macomb Intermediate School District and Leaps & Bounds Family Services. We joined together as a collaborative and collectively applied for and received Social Innovation Fund (SIF) resources, through a partnership with United Way for Southeastern Michigan. The advantages of working together have been immense.

Macomb Family Services cannot express enough gratitude for the work that David Crumm has put into making this book an engaging and informative look into the social-emotional lives of children and how we can positively influence them. David's interviewing skills, journalism expertise and vision are remarkable. We couldn't have produced the book efficiently without the organizational skills and enthusiasm that Shaun Taft brought to the project, keeping us all on task, focused and excited. Also, thank you to Rebecca Tallarigo and Lindsey Miller, the artists whose work appears in these pages—and to the Front Edge Publishing team of Dmitri Barvinok, Celeste Dykas and Stephanie Fenton. And thank you to other staff members at Macomb Family Services who supported us behind the scenes. Wayne Baker, Kathleen Macdonald, Robert J. Wicks, Ben Pratt and Alicia Guevara Warren took time to add insight to ideas unfolding throughout the book. Finally, thank you to all of the other professionals and families (too many to name) who gave of their time for interviews that added so much to our book and our work! We are grateful to you for helping us share the message of relationships and social-emotional development.

The importance and impact of relationships in our work is the focus of this book. Therefore, this acknowledgement section wouldn't be the same if we didn't give thanks to the relationships that helped shape our work and who we are in that work.

From Christine Zimmerman

Many people and relationships in my life have a profound influence on who I am as a person and as a social worker. I want to thank Barb Broesamle, who gave me a solid foundation in ethics, confidentiality, strengths perspectives, reflective practice and, most importantly, showed me that relationship is everything. I also want to thank Laureen Niehaus-Beckner and Blair Schoen, who always had the best interest of families in mind. They never let politics interfere with best practices for families and children. Most importantly, they taught me the value of collaboration. Collaboration is the building of relationships that starts with our self-growth and reflection—focused on what we bring to them rather than focusing on what we get out of them. We have a greater impact together! Blair had a strong influence in growing my program management skills founded in the same parallel process as our work with families. And I want to thank Kate Merrilees, who strengthened and supported my work with families through growing my reflective practice. Kate provided space for growing self-awareness, support, and the deep reflection of my learning and growth regarding my clinical work with families. Carolyn McKanders joined my journey at a time when I was ready to deepen my work and take it to a new level. I am so appreciative to all of those who have supported my growth and development and my hope is that this book is one way I can pay it forward to others.

From Alejandra Medina

Working with relationships could be a thing that, if taken too seriously, could feel overwhelming. That is why I like to add a taste of playfulness and a sense of humor as much as possible. Teachers, parents and students learn that getting along can be an easy task if it is enjoyed. For this reason, I would like to thank my main teacher in this—my mentor in the art of play, enjoyment, being genuine and being in the moment—my dad, who showed me that getting along is a matter of joy and not something that should be forced to happen. His influence is a constant reminder of freshness, spontaneity and love. My other mentor has been my mother, who showed me perseverance, strength, commitment and a love to care for others. Both of my parents, in their own way, have shown me they are that important person in my life that has made a difference for me. These role models provided the frame of reference I use when I interact with others and provide me with the skills that help me to make a difference in someone else's life.

From Bronwyn Johnston

I would like to acknowledge two teams of coworkers with whom I have been lucky enough to work. First, I would like to acknowledge the Foster Care and Child Protective Services teams at Baltimore County Department of Social Services. Although every worker was under an incredible amount of stress they pulled together daily to support each other in any and every way. In such a tumultuous position, it is essential to one's sense of self and mental well-being to know that such a group of caring peers has your back. Second, I would like to acknowledge the team at Macomb Family Services. I entered the agency as a relatively new mom, returning to the workforce in a new state, completely detached from the support system I had known. I was lucky enough to find another great set of peers who consistently step up and help one another. This book focuses on the impact of building relationships and all of you are proof that relationships among people make all the difference!

From La Don Williams

The relationships and opportunities in my life have not come by chance; I believe that they have been divine appointments from God. Relationships are important and they require work in order to be maintained. When working with or parenting young children, a support system of people who are vested in your success, as well as the child's, is essential. My mom, Eliza Stewart, is one of my greatest inspirations, because of her love and time spent with me; I was able to bounce back from being abandoned as a newborn. I can still remember the songs and finger plays she recited to comfort and teach me. She also taught me how to be patient, respectful and nonjudgmental of others. Sherie Posie has also been instrumental in helping me with my own parenting skills. She offered support, understanding and encouragement when I needed it and gave me practical strategies and techniques to use when I was faced with challenging situations. Carol Nardin, my first mentor in early childhood education, taught me how to be an intentional teacher: to see from the child's perspective and to provide young children with opportunities to explore, experiment and learn, all while creating a love for learning. These relationships serve as models to help me communicate to families and care providers that children need their love, respect, hugs, guidance, encouragement and presence.

Finally, this book would not have been possible without the support of the Ready Children/Ready Community Collaborative, United Way for Southeastern Michigan, and the Corporation for National and Community Service.

About the Authors

As this book was prepared:

Christine Zimmerman, a licensed master social worker (LMSW), is the director of early childhood programming at Macomb Family Services in Macomb County. Her expertise includes work with children and families in a variety of roles such as family education and support, child welfare, diversity, ethics and community engagement and collaboration. In addition to her work as a social worker and administrator, she is an educator and author of the book, *Tell Me About God Again*. Christine is passionate about supporting quality work with families and children and she mentors others to support families using effective, culturally sensitive practice. Christine is an adjunct social work professor at Oakland University in Rochester, Michigan. She is a national trainer for Parents as Teachers, a proven home-visiting model that supports the evolving needs of families so that their young children can grow up healthy, safe and ready to learn. Christine is always eager to learn and to support others in their own learning process because she believes that every human being can excel in their journey through life if somebody believes in them.

> Christine's mission statement: To provide a supportive, peaceful environment where everyone can grow, feel hope, and have the tools they need to provide quality, meaningful services to the community.

Alejandra Medina, a limited licensed professional counselor (LLPC) and national certified counselor (NCC) is a social-emotional consultant at Macomb Family Services. A graduate from Oakland University, she is committed to supporting families' development and to improve their mental well-being. As part of this commitment, it is very important for her to work with the early childhood population, to both promote protective factors at an early age and to identify risk factors that could be modified or redirected. Alejandra has 10 years of experience working with the early childhood population as a home visitor, program developer and as a therapist. Alejandra's passion is to support people's awakening to their hidden strengths and passions—something that will eventually lead them to live their lives in a fuller, happier and more mindful way.

> Alejandra's mission statement: To promote people's growth (including mine) in a genuine and proactive way.

Bronwyn Johnston (LMSW) is a social-emotional consultant at Macomb Family Services. She received her bachelor's degree in social work from Western Maryland College in 2000 and received her master's in social work from West Virginia University in 2002. She worked in both private and public foster care following graduation. She worked in foster care for seven years, specializing in young children, children with disabilities and drug-exposed newborns. Following her time with foster care, Bronwyn worked in Child Protective Services for three years and for one year with Family Preservation Services. Upon moving to Michigan, Bronwyn joined the social-emotional team at

Macomb Family Services. She has been a social-emotional consultant for over two years.

La Don Williams is a supervisor and an early childhood specialist/parent educator at Macomb Family Services Early Learning Communities. She has worked in this field of educating families and those who care for young children for over 25 years, in different aspects. She has worked with Macomb Family Services for five years and has successfully helped to increase enrollment in Play and Learn groups. She received her Bachelor of Science in early childhood education at Baker College.

> La Don's mission statement: To assist, model and provide support to caregivers and parents, with information and resources on age-appropriate practices for young children as they develop skills for kindergarten and the joy of learning.

Owen Pfaendtner is president and CEO of Macomb Family Services. He is a licensed social worker. As CEO, Owen's responsibilities include strategic planning, fund development, board development, fiscal management and program and organizational development. Owen is one of three founding members of Family Service Alliance for Southeastern Michigan, a collaboration of three family service agencies designed to increase capacity and quality of services to children and families in the Detroit Tri-County Area. He also has been involved in other regional collaboratives, including the Southeast Michigan Senior Regional Collaborative and the Macomb County Provider Alliance. Owen and his wife, Donna, have been married for 27 years and they reside with their children, Stephen, Matthew and Alexandria, in Bruce Township, Michigan.

The Bib to Backpack Learning Series

Join us in giving children a great start! Remember: Education begins before school. Research shows that the years between the bib and the backpack make all the difference for school readiness and lifelong success. So, let's make those years count!

That's our goal at United Way for Southeastern Michigan in launching this new campaign we call Bib to Backpack. A wide range of informational resources are available for parents and caregivers online at: www.BibToBackpack.org

In addition, this Learning Series within the campaign will expand into six individual books throughout 2016, highlighting the inspiring and innovative programs we are sponsoring through the Corporation for National and Community Service's Social Innovation Fund. Sharing these programs with other communities is a major goal of that fund's important work nationwide. We hope that the stories, voices and resources in these books will inspire parents, students, community leaders and professionals nationwide who are looking for fresh ideas to prepare children for school.

Call to Action

If this book has inspired you and you would like to learn more about the work described here, please contact Macomb Family Services at: www.mfsonline.org

You may also contact Christine Zimmerman at:

Macomb Family Services
36975 Utica Rd, Suite 102
Clinton Township, MI 48036
elcprogram@gmail.com

CPSIA information can be obtained
at www.ICGtesting.com
Printed in the USA
LVOW01s1951141016
508383LV00004B/6/P

9 781942 011576